FOR ORGANS, PIANOS & ELECTRONIC KEYBOARDS

E-Z PLAY TODAY

243

Oldies! Oldies! Oldies!

ISBN 978-0-634-03349-0

HAL•LEONARD®
CORPORATION
7777 W. BLUEMOUND RD. P.O. BOX 13819 MILWAUKEE, WI 53213

E-Z Play® Today Music Notation © 1975 by HAL LEONARD CORPORATION
E-Z PLAY and EASY ELECTRONIC KEYBOARD MUSIC are registered trademarks of HAL LEONARD CORPORATION.

Visit Hal Leonard Online at
www.halleonard.com

Oldies! Oldies! Oldies!

Barbara Ann

Registration 7
Rhythm: Rock

Words and Music by
Fred Fassert

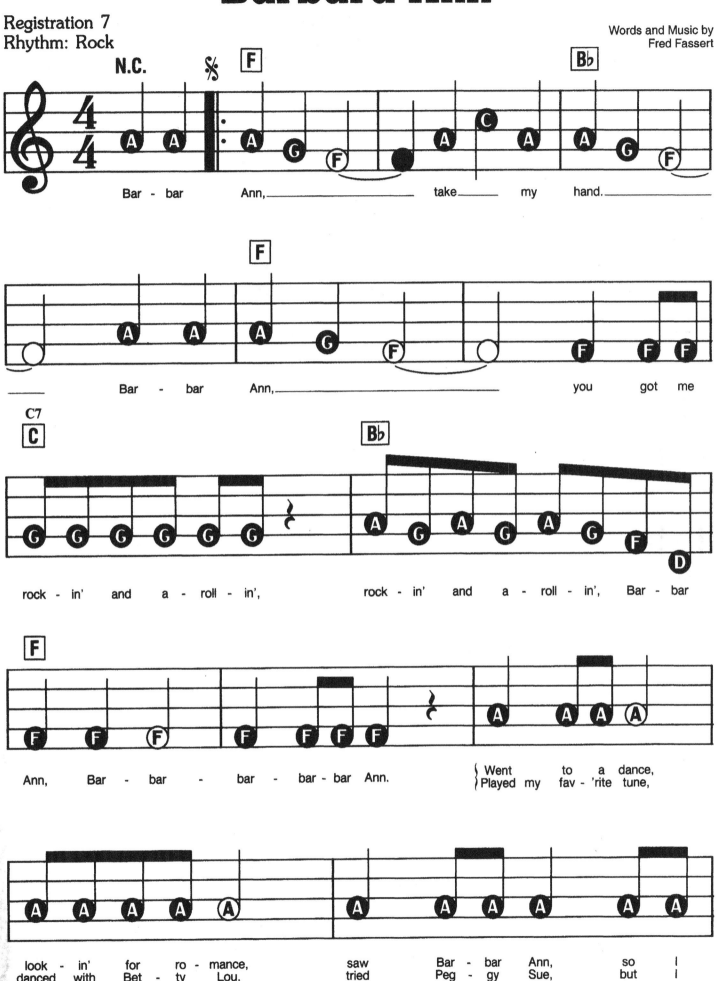

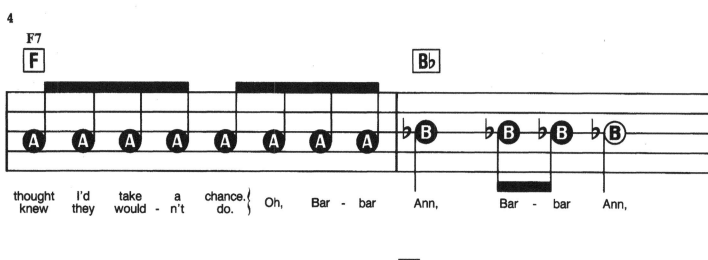

thought I'd take a chance.
knew they would-n't do. } Oh, Bar - bar Ann, Bar - bar Ann,

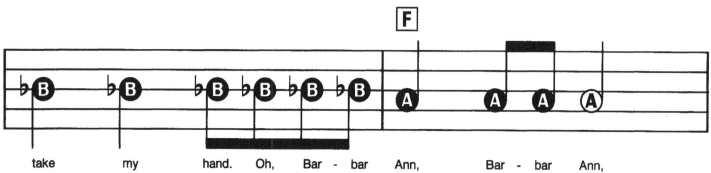

take my hand. Oh, Bar - bar Ann, Bar - bar Ann,

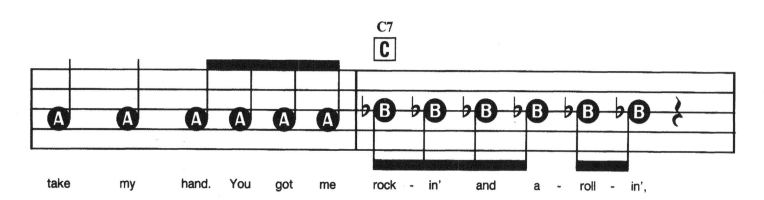

take my hand. You got me rock - in' and a - roll - in',

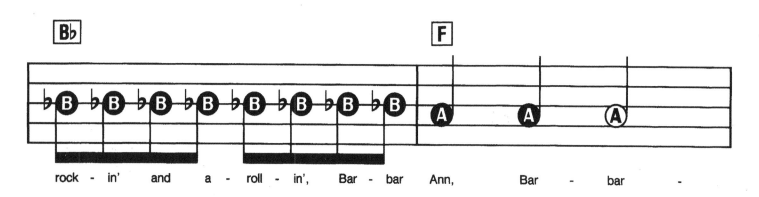

rock - in' and a - roll - in', Bar - bar Ann, Bar - bar -

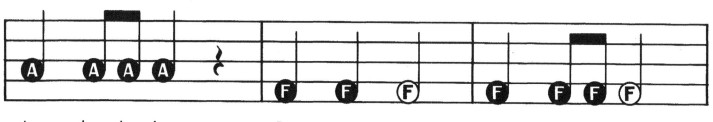

bar - bar-bar Ann. Bar - bar Ann, Bar - bar-bar Ann,

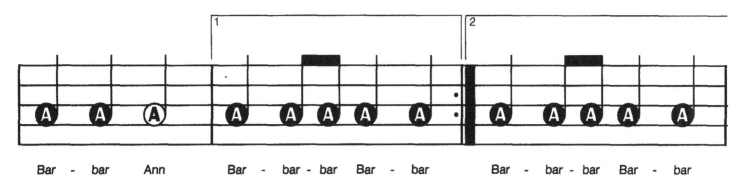

Bar - bar Ann   Bar - bar - bar Bar - bar   Bar - bar - bar Bar - bar

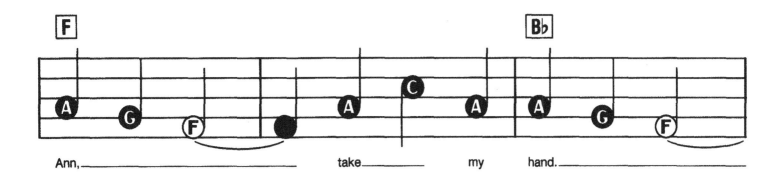

Ann, _____ take _____ my hand. _____

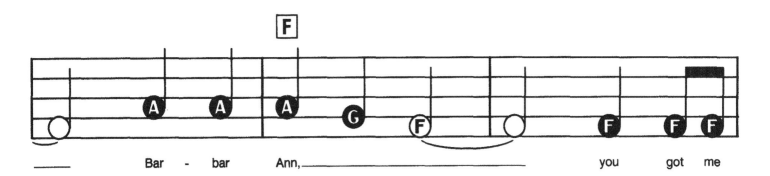

_____ Bar - bar Ann, _____ you got me

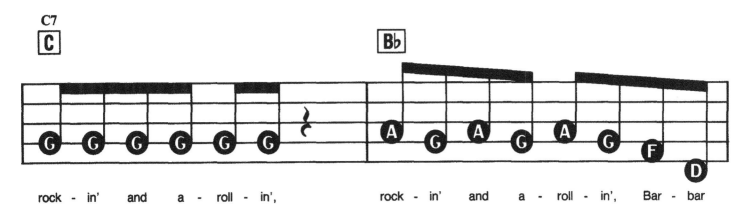

rock - in' and a - roll - in',   rock - in' and a - roll - in', Bar - bar

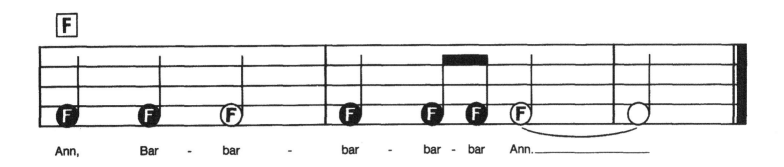

Ann,   Bar - bar - bar - bar - bar Ann. _____

Cathy's Clown

Registration 1
Rhythm: Pops or 8 Beat

Words and Music by
Don Everly

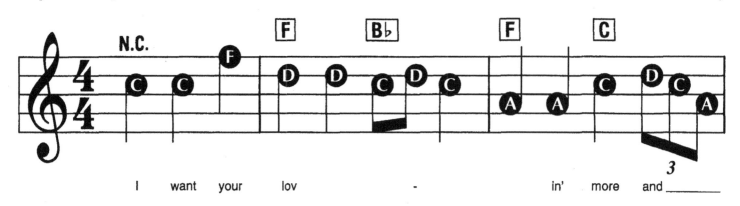

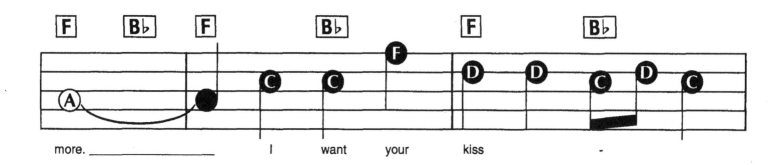

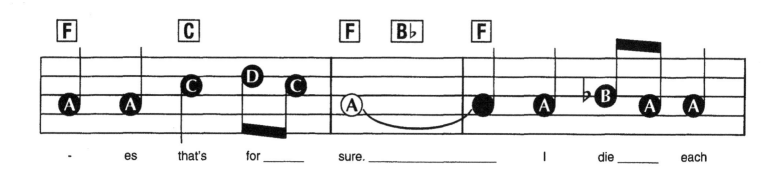

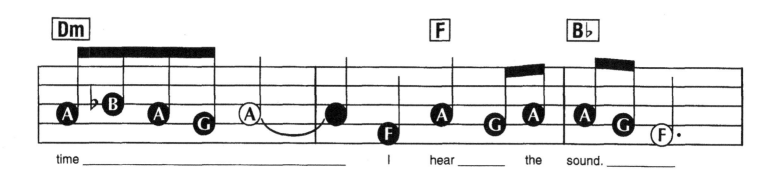

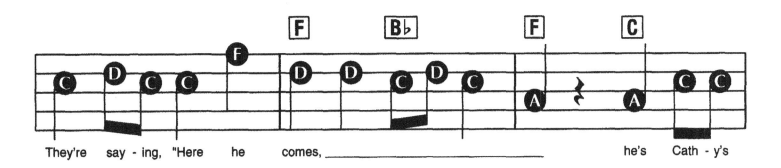

They're say - ing, "Here he comes, _____ he's Cath - y's

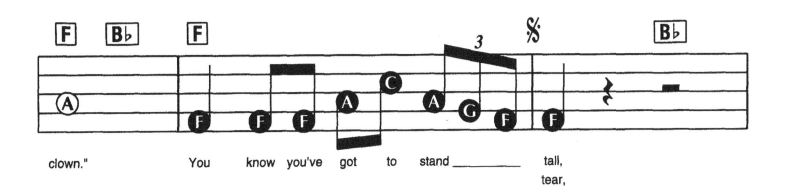

clown." You know you've got to stand _____ tall,
tear,

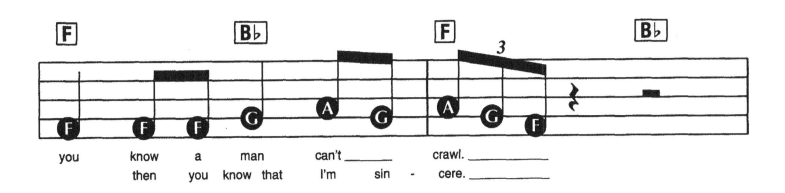

you know a man can't _____ crawl. _____
then you know that I'm sin - cere. _____

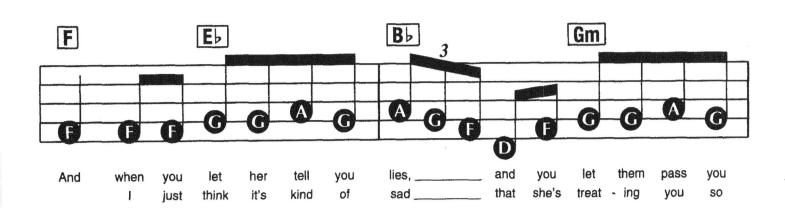

And when you let her tell you lies, _____ and you let them pass you
I just think it's kind of sad _____ that she's treat - ing you so

To Coda ⊕

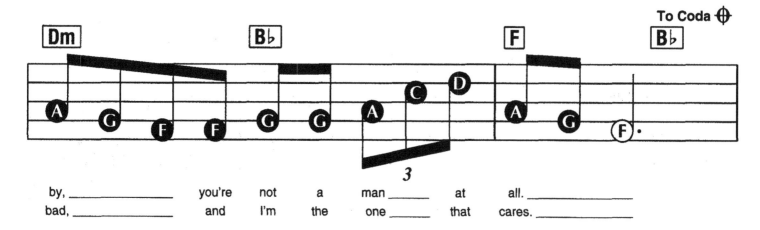

by, _____ you're not a man _____ at all. _____
bad, _____ and I'm the one _____ that cares. _____

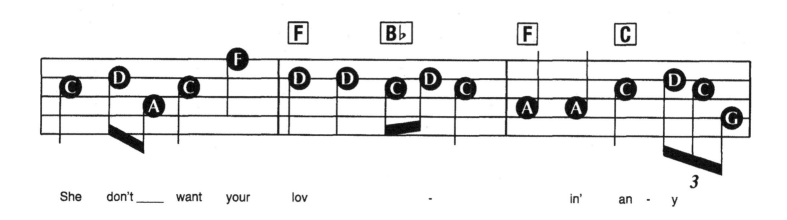

She don't ____ want your lov - in' an - y

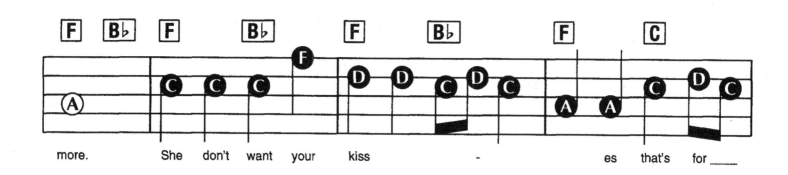

more. She don't want your kiss - es that's for ____

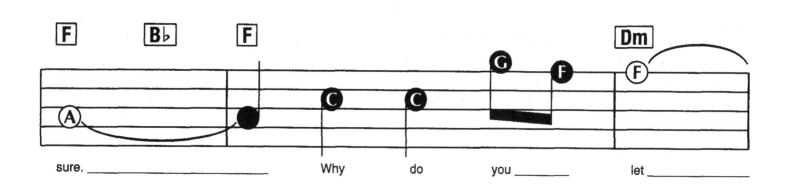

sure. _____ Why do you _____ let _____

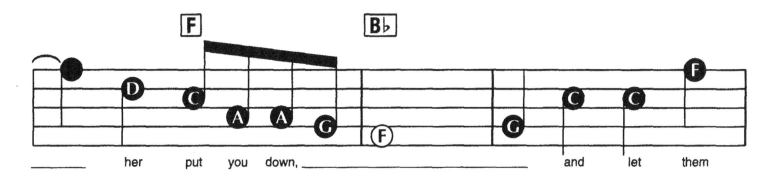

_____ her put you down, _____ and let them

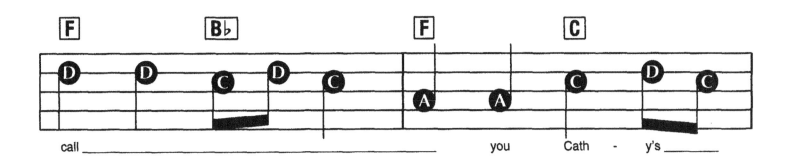

call _____ you Cath - y's _____

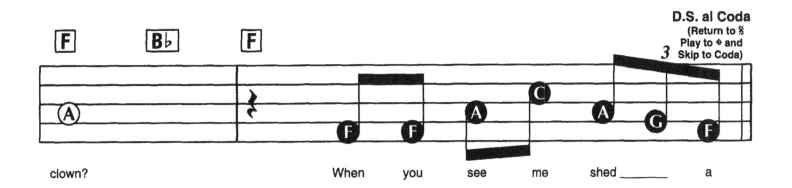

clown? When you see me shed _____ a

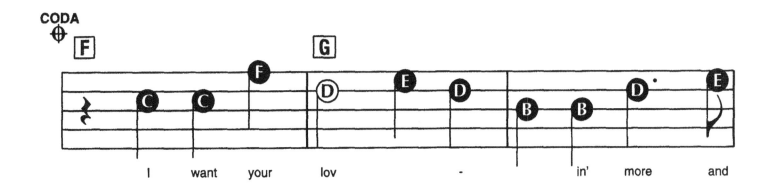

I want your lov - in' more and

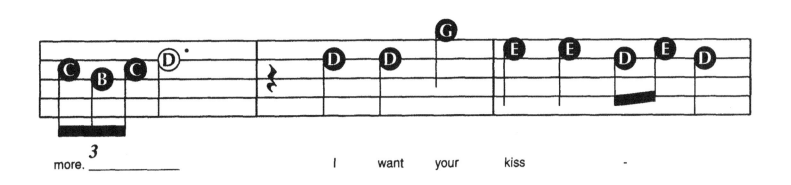

more. _____ I want your kiss -

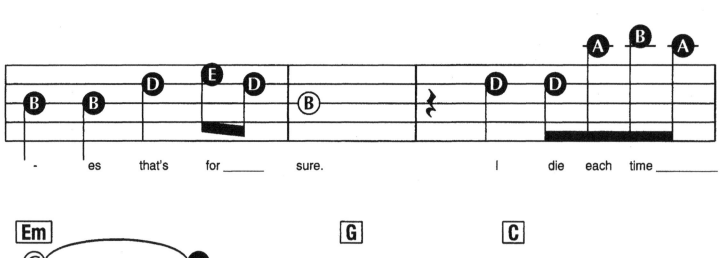

- es   that's   for _____ sure.   I   die   each   time _____

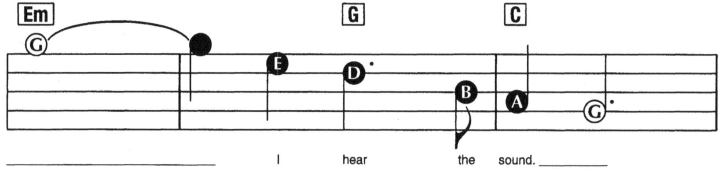

_____   I   hear   the   sound. _____

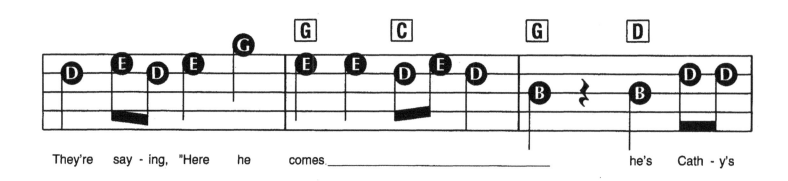

They're   say - ing, "Here   he   comes._____   he's   Cath - y's

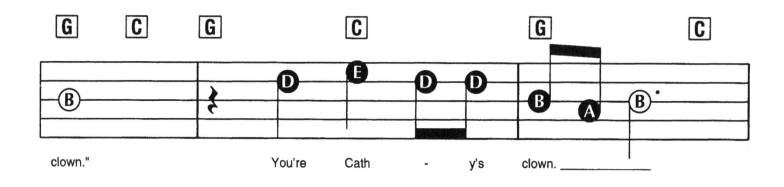

clown."   You're   Cath - y's   clown. _____

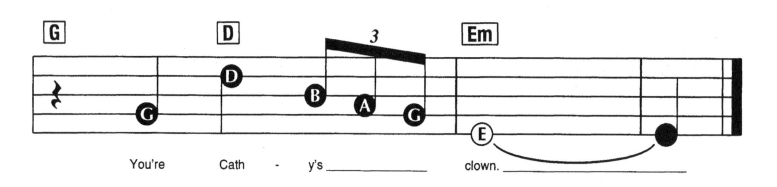

You're   Cath - y's _____   clown. _____

Crying

Registration 3
Rhythm: Country Ballad

Words and Music by Roy Orbison
and Joe Melson

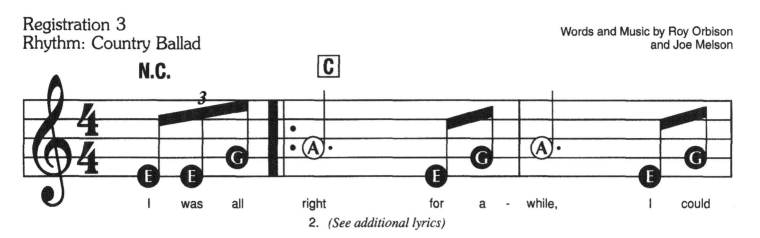

2. *(See additional lyrics)*

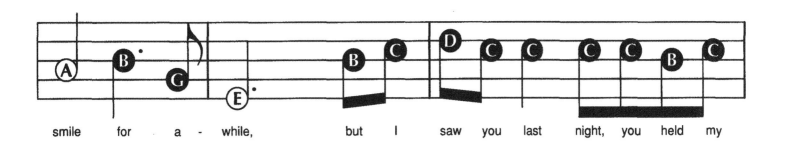

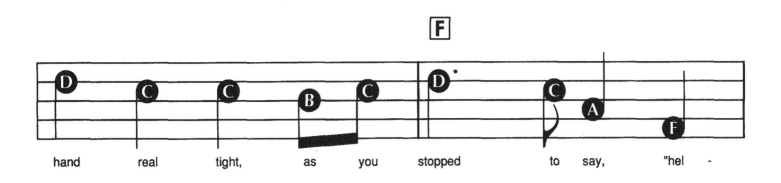

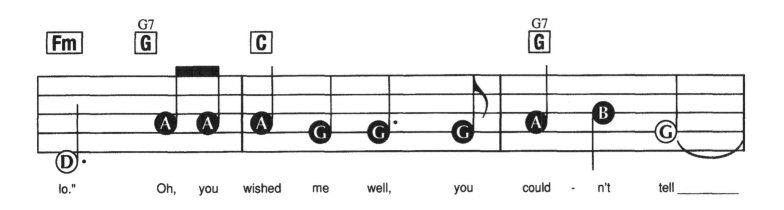

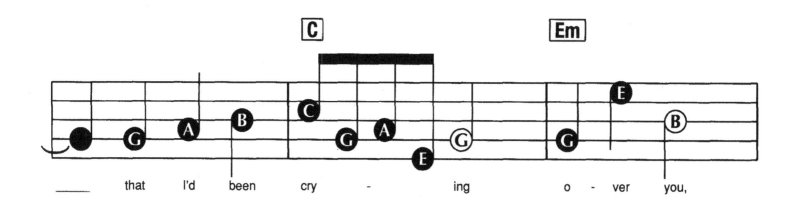

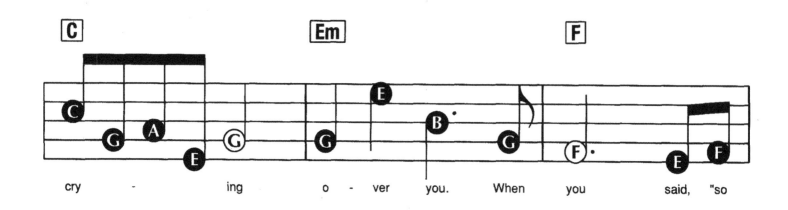

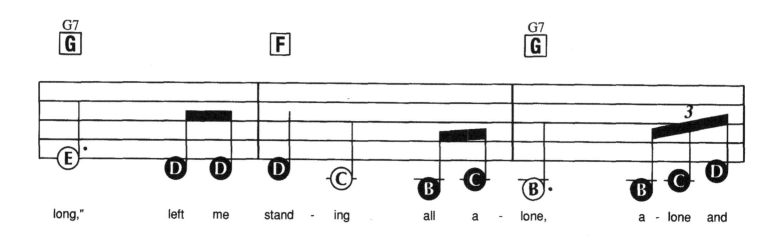

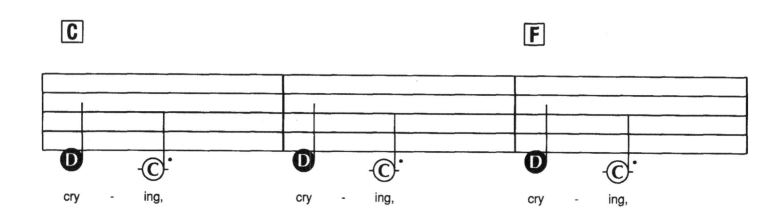

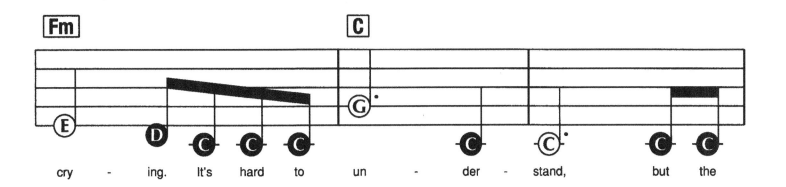

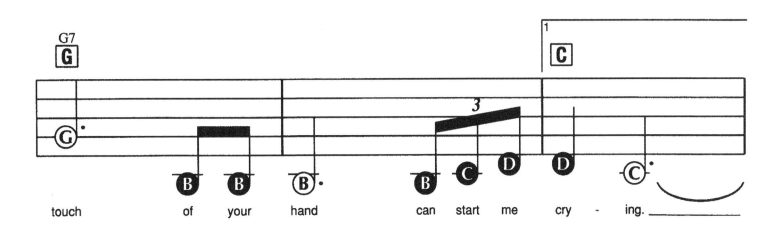

cry - ing. It's hard to un - der - stand, but the

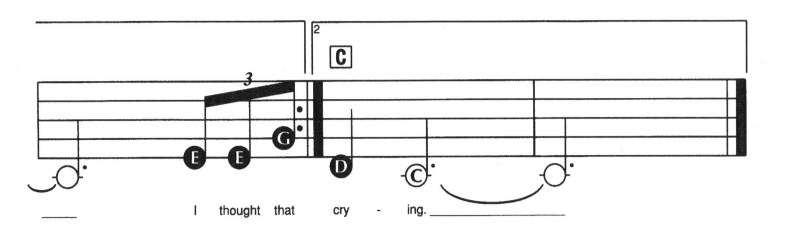

touch of your hand can start me cry - ing. _____

_____ I thought that cry - ing. _____

Additional Lyrics

2   I thought that I was over you,
    But it's true, so true:
    I love you even more than I did before.
    But darling, what can I do?
    For you don't love me and I'll always be
    Crying over you, crying over you.
    Yes, now you're gone and from this moment on
    I'll be crying, crying, crying, crying,
    Yeah, crying, crying over you.

Dizzy

Registration 1
Rhythm: 8 Beat or Rock

Words and Music by Tommy Roe
and Freddy Weller

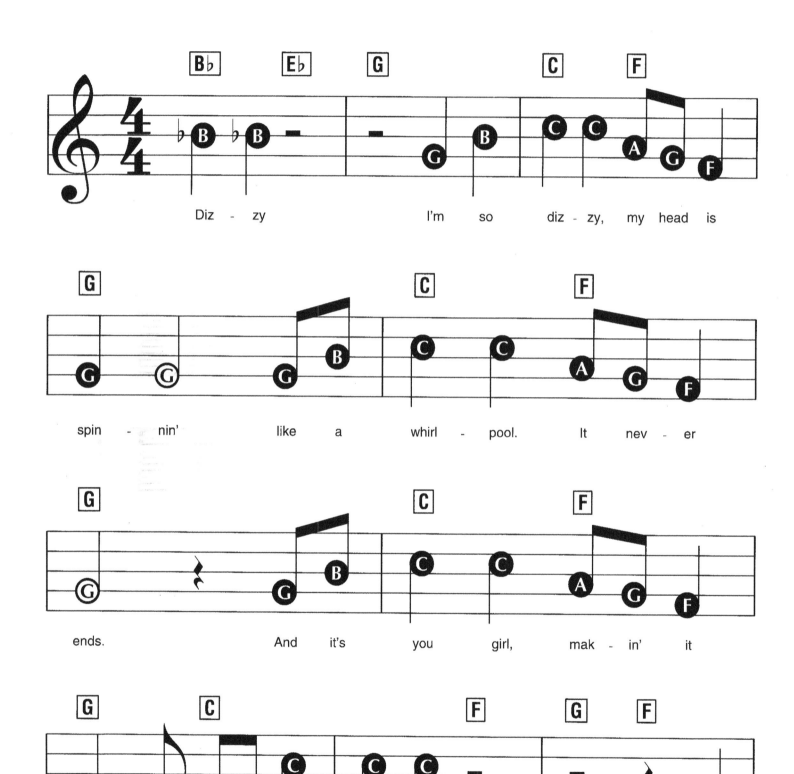

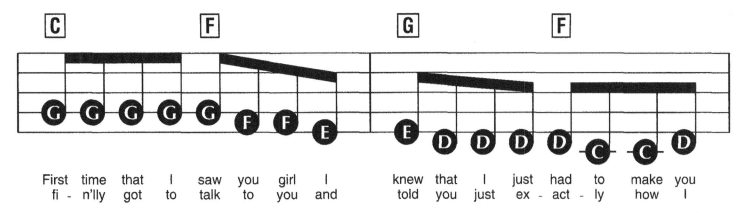

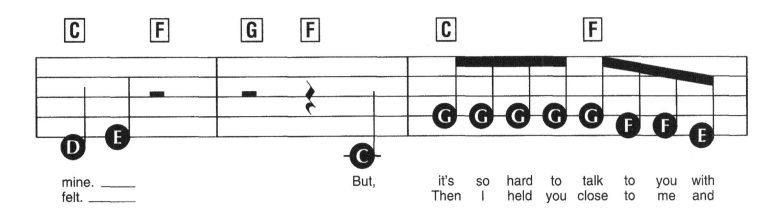

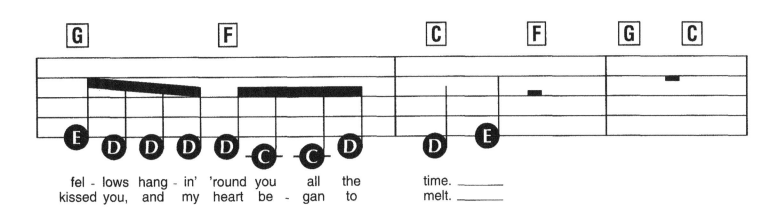

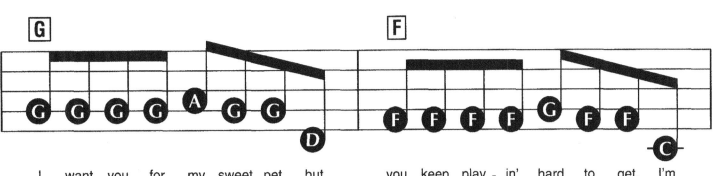

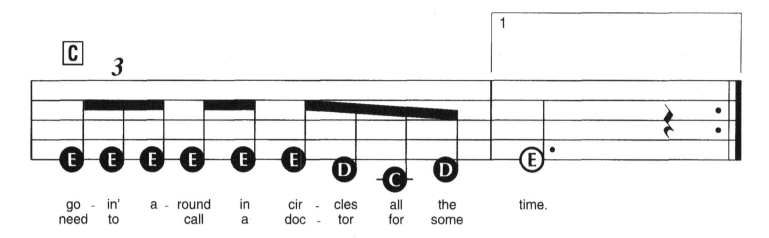

go - in' a - round in cir - cles all the time.
need to call a doc - tor for some

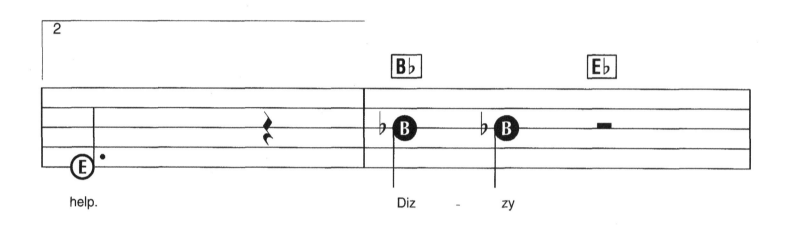

help. Diz - zy

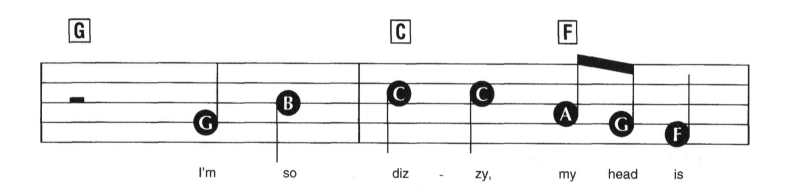

I'm so diz - zy, my head is

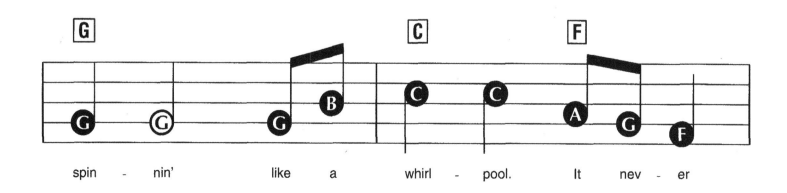

spin - nin' like a whirl - pool. It nev - er

17

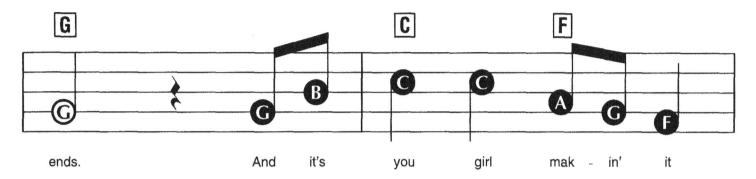

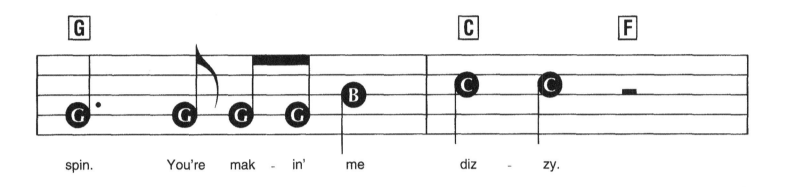

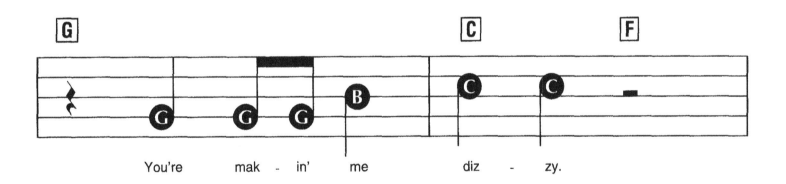

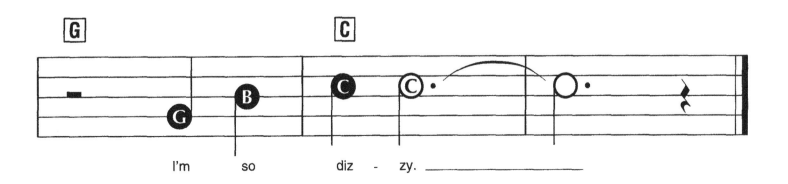

(Sittin' On)
The Dock of the Bay

Registration 5
Rhythm: Rock

Words and Music by Steve Cropper
and Otis Redding

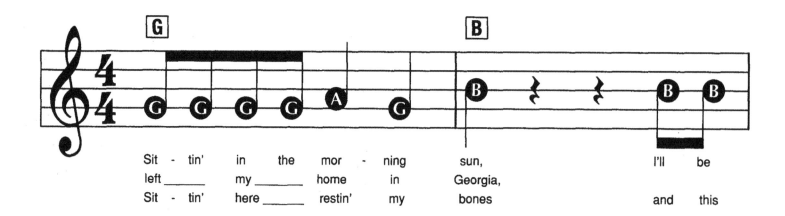

Sit - tin' in the mor - ning sun,   I'll be
left ____ my ____ home in Georgia,
Sit - tin' here ____ restin' my bones   and this

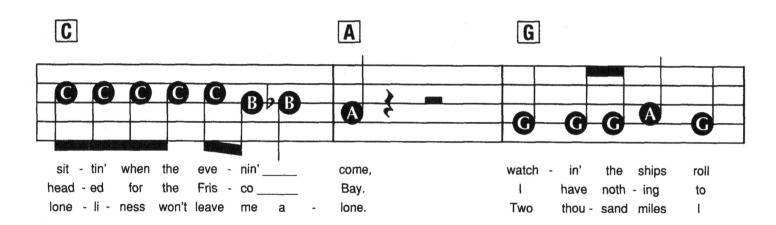

sit - tin' when the eve - nin' ____ come,   watch - in' the ships roll
head - ed for the Fris - co ____ Bay.   I have noth - ing to
lone - li - ness won't leave me a - lone.   Two thou - sand miles I

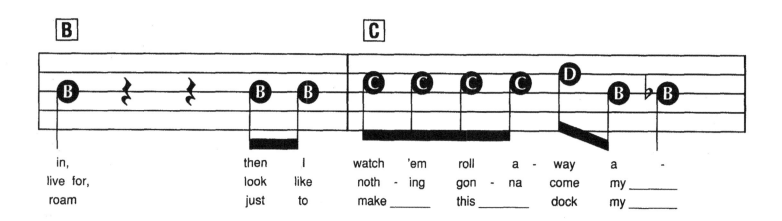

in,   then I watch 'em roll a - way a -
live for,   look like noth - ing gon - na come my ____
roam   just to make ____ this ____ dock my ____

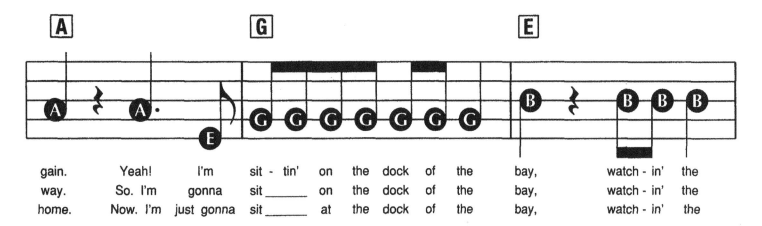

gain.   Yeah!   I'm   sit - tin'   on   the   dock   of   the   bay,   watch - in'   the
way.   So. I'm   gonna   sit ____ on   the   dock   of   the   bay,   watch - in'   the
home.   Now. I'm   just gonna   sit ____ at   the   dock   of   the   bay,   watch - in'   the

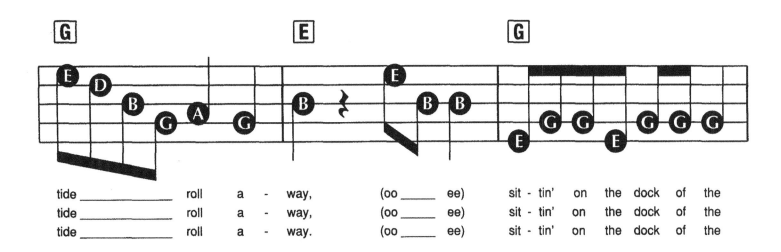

tide ____ roll   a - way,   (oo __ ee)   sit - tin'   on   the   dock   of   the
tide ____ roll   a - way,   (oo __ ee)   sit - tin'   on   the   dock   of   the
tide ____ roll   a - way.   (oo __ ee)   sit - tin'   on   the   dock   of   the

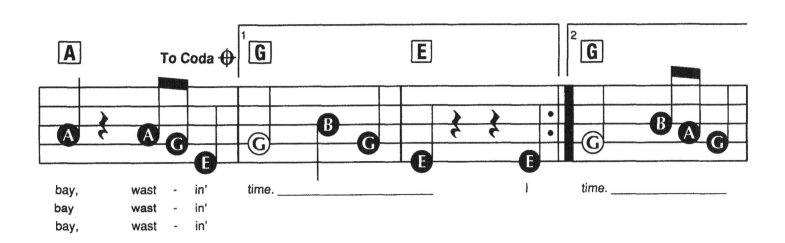

bay,   wast - in'   time. _____   I   time. _____
bay   wast - in'
bay,   wast - in'

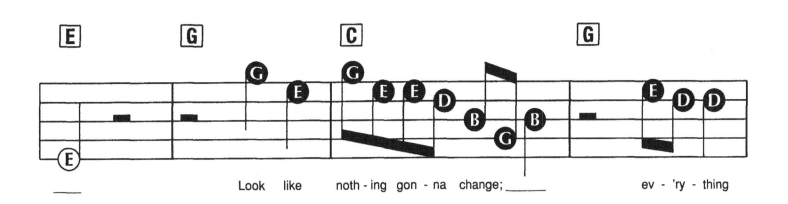

____   Look   like   noth - ing gon - na change; ____   ev - 'ry - thing

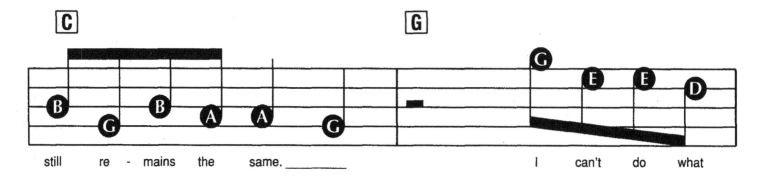

still re - mains the same. _____ I can't do what

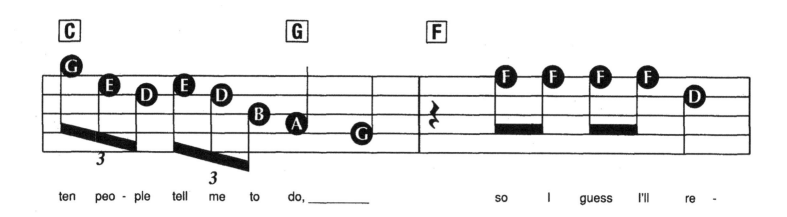

ten peo - ple tell me to do, _____ so I guess I'll re -

D.C. al Coda
(Return to beginning
Play to ⊕ and
Skip to Coda)

CODA

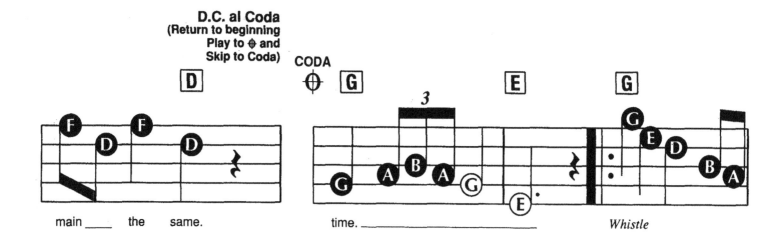

main ____ the same.

time. _____

Whistle

Repeat and Fade

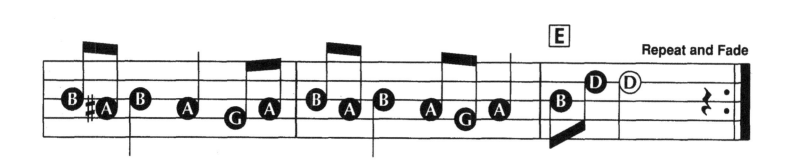

Games People Play

Registration 4
Rhythm: Country

Words and Music by
Joe South

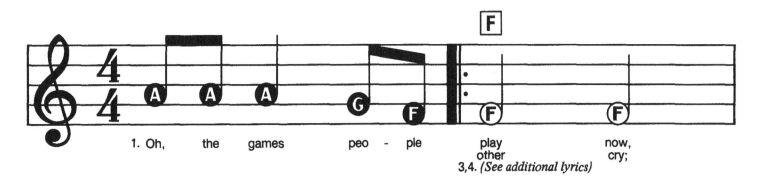

1. Oh,   the   games   peo - ple   play   now,
other   cry;
3,4. *(See additional lyrics)*

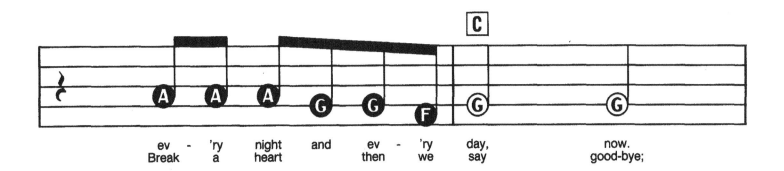

ev - 'ry   night   and   ev - 'ry   day,   now.
Break   a   heart   then   we   say   good-bye;

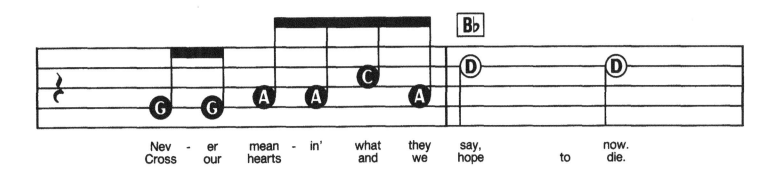

Nev - er   mean - in'   what   they   say,   now.
Cross   our   hearts   and   we   hope   to   die.

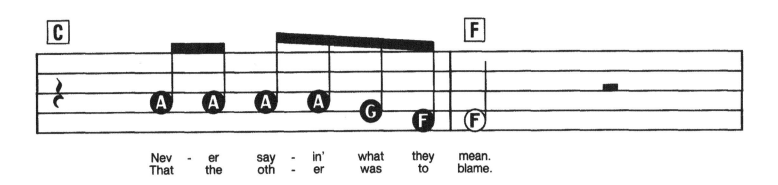

Nev - er   say - in'   what   they   mean.
That   the   oth - er   was   to   blame.

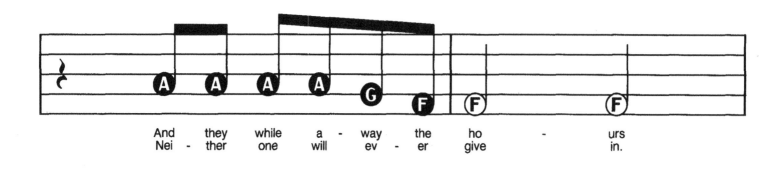

And they while a - way the ho - urs
Nei - ther one will ev - er give in.

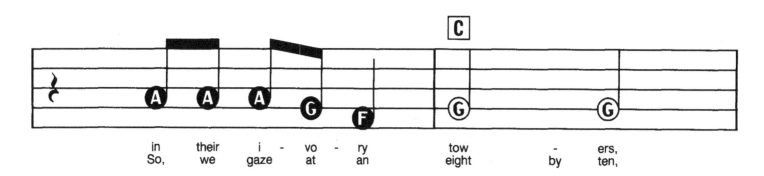

in their i - vo - ry tow - ers,
So, we gaze at an eight by ten,

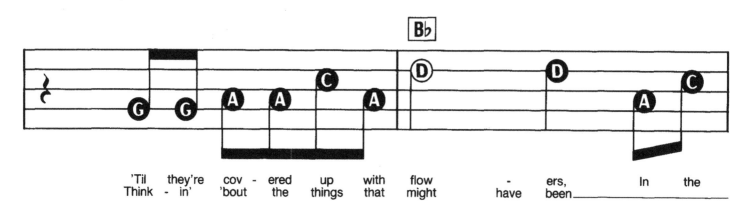

'Til they're cov - ered up with flow - ers, In the
Think - in' 'bout the things that might have been

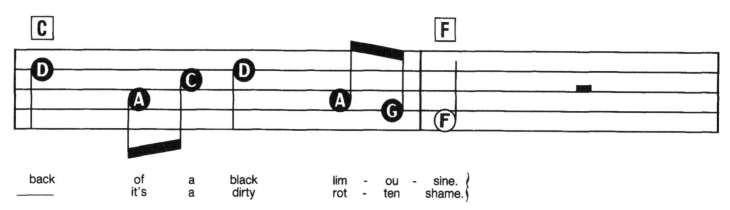

back of a black lim - ou - sine.
it's a dirty rot - ten shame.

CHORUS

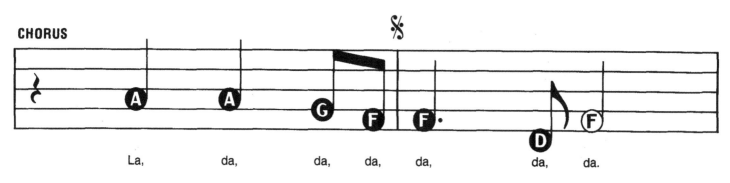

La, da, da, da, da, da, da.

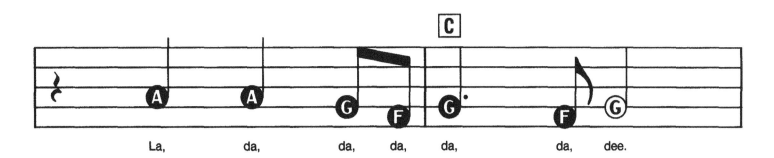

La, da, da, da, da, da, dee.

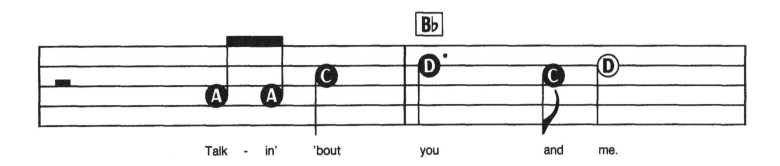

Talk - in' 'bout you and me.

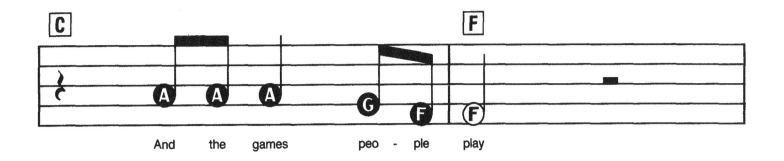

And the games peo - ple play

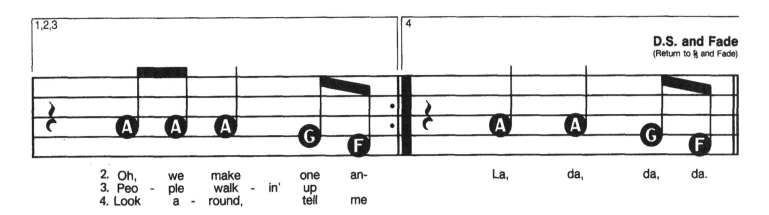

2. Oh, we make one an-
3. Peo - ple walk - in' up
4. Look a - round, tell me

La, da, da, da.

D.S. and Fade
(Return to % and Fade)

Additional lyrics

3. People walkin up to you
Singin' "Glory Hallelujah!"
And they're tryin' to sock it to ya
In the name of the Lord.
They gonna teach you how to meditate,
Read your horoscope and cheat your fate,
And furthermore to hell with hate.
Come on get on board.

Chorus

4. Look around, tell me what you see.
What's happenin' to you and me?
God grant me the serenity
To remember who I am.
'Cause you're givin' up your sanity
For your pride and your vanity.
Turn your back on humanity,
And don't give a da da da da da.

Chorus

Down in the Boondocks

Registration 1
Rhythm: 8 Beat or Rock

Words and Music by
Joe South

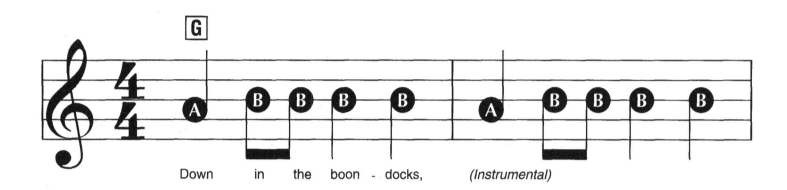

Down in the boon - docks, *(Instrumental)*

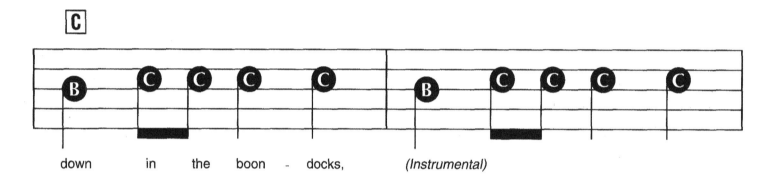

down in the boon - docks, *(Instrumental)*

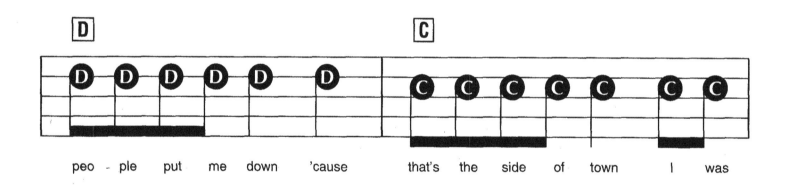

peo - ple put me down 'cause   that's the side of town I was

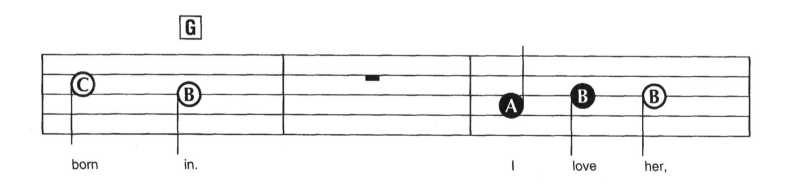

born in.   I love her,

25

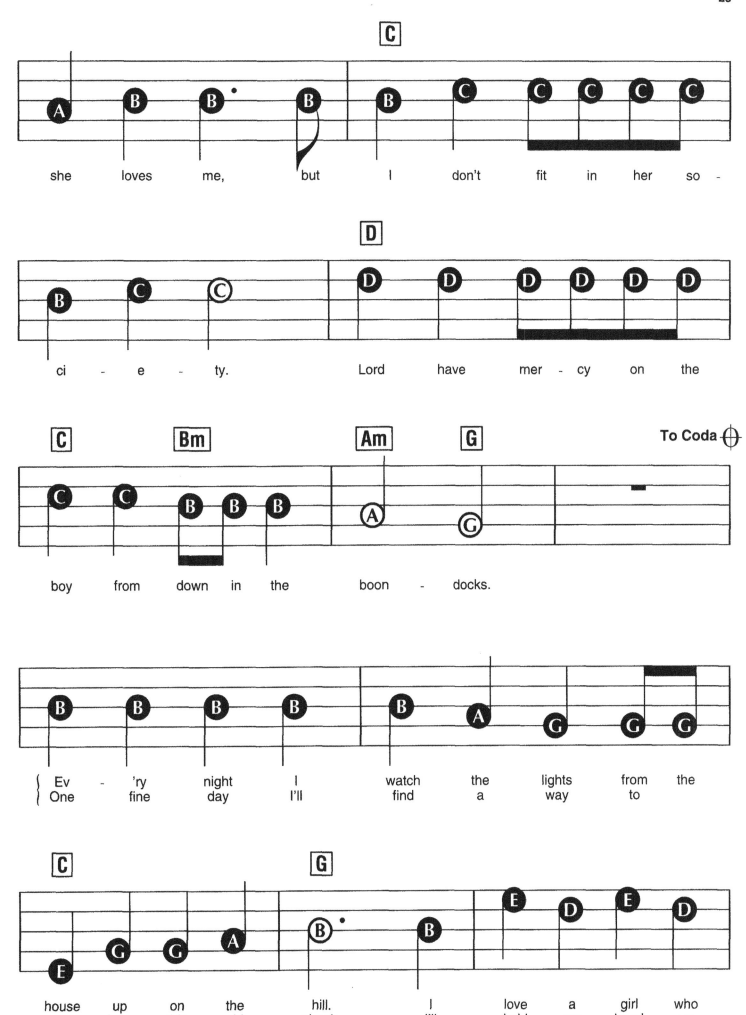

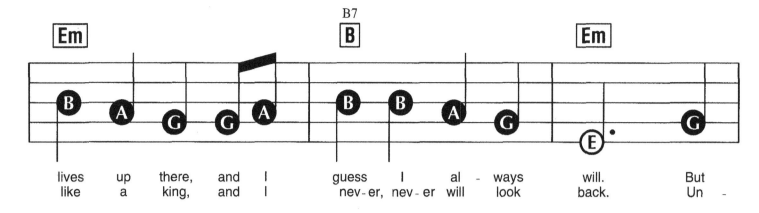

lives up there, and I | guess I al - ways will. But
like a king, and and I | nev - er, nev - er will look back. Un -

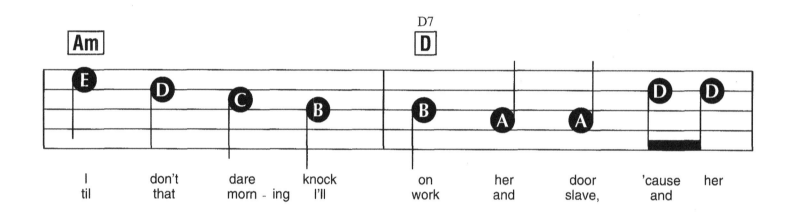

I don't dare knock | on her door, 'cause her
til that morn - ing I'll | work and slave, and

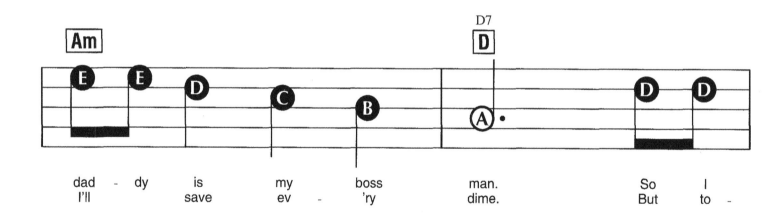

dad - dy is my boss | man. So I
I'll save ev - 'ry | dime. But to -

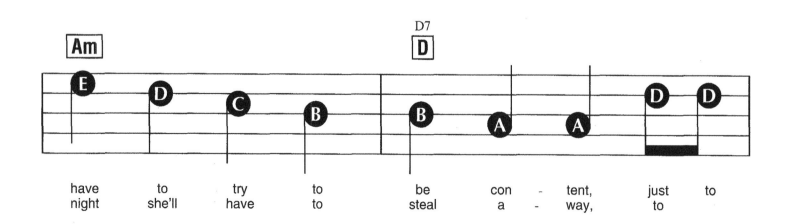

have to try to | be con - tent, just to
night she'll have to | steal a - way, to

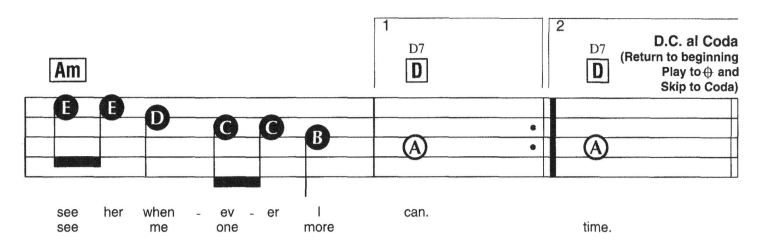

see her when - ev - er I can.
see me one more time.

D.C. al Coda
(Return to beginning
Play to ⊕ and
Skip to Coda)

CODA

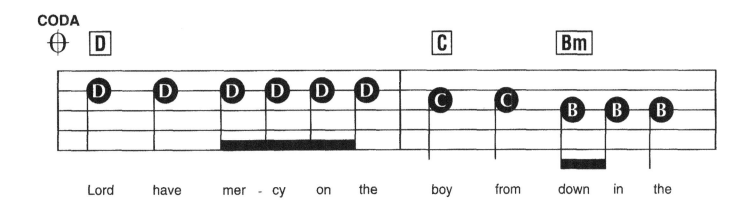

Lord have mer - cy on the boy from down in the

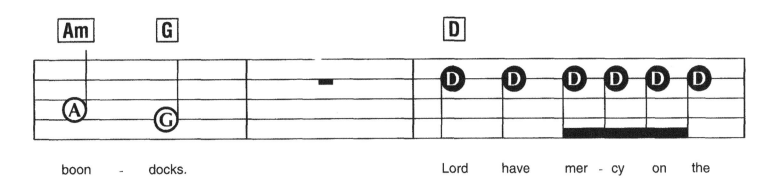

boon - docks. Lord have mer - cy on the

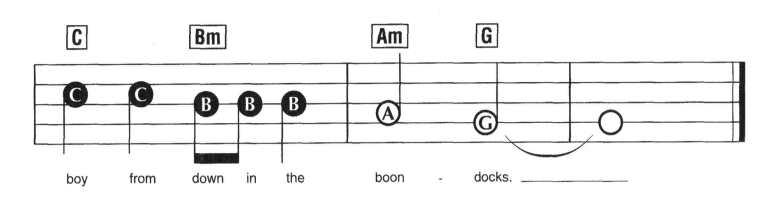

boy from down in the boon - docks. _____

Get a Job

Registration 4
Rhythm: Rock or 8 Beat

Words and Music by Earl Beal, Richard Lewis,
Raymond Edwards and William Horton

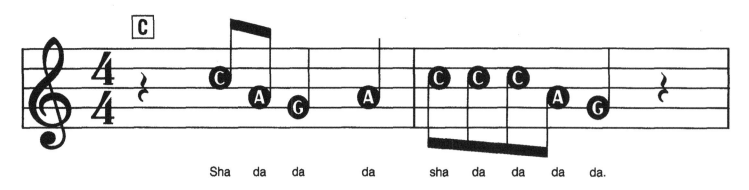

Sha da da da sha da da da da.

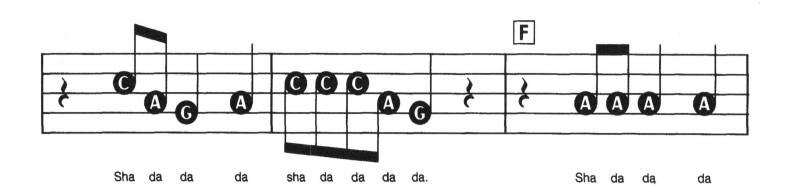

Sha da da da sha da da da da. Sha da da da

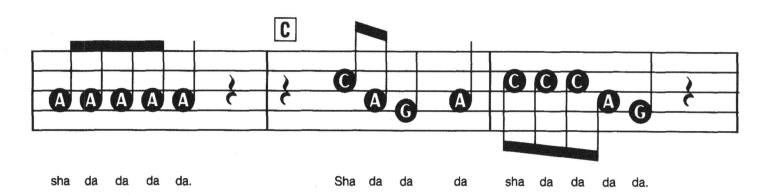

sha da da da da. Sha da da da sha da da da da.

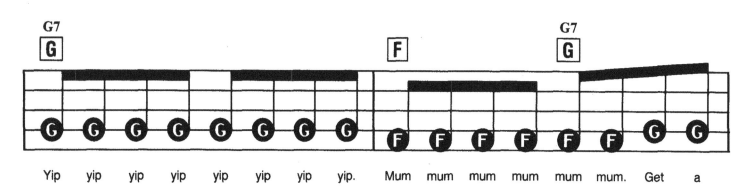

Yip yip yip yip yip yip yip yip. Mum mum mum mum mum mum. Get a

29

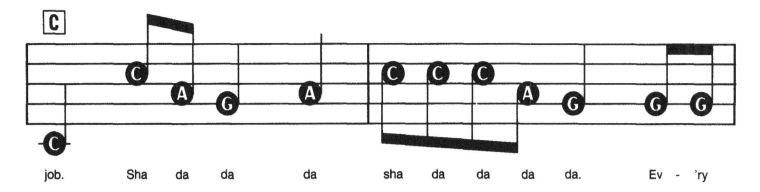

job. Sha da da da sha da da da da. Ev - 'ry

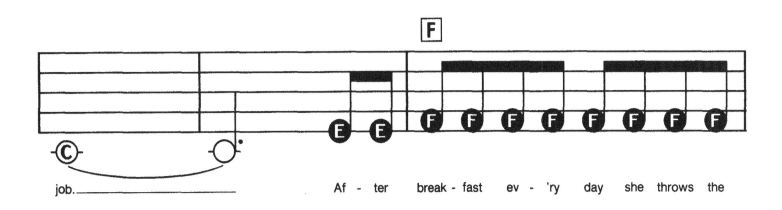

morn - ing a - bout this time she get me out of my bed a - cry - ing get a

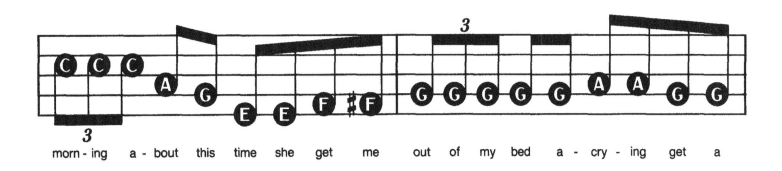

job._____ Af - ter break - fast ev - 'ry day she throws the

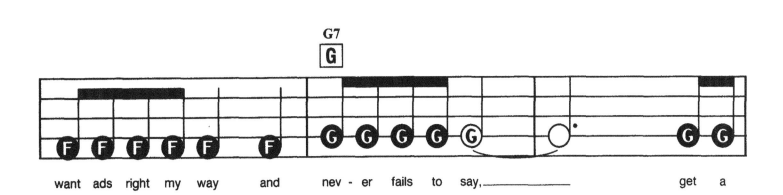

want ads right my way and nev - er fails to say,_____ get a

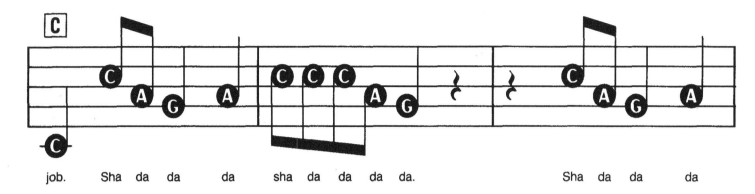

job. Sha da da da sha da da da da. Sha da da da

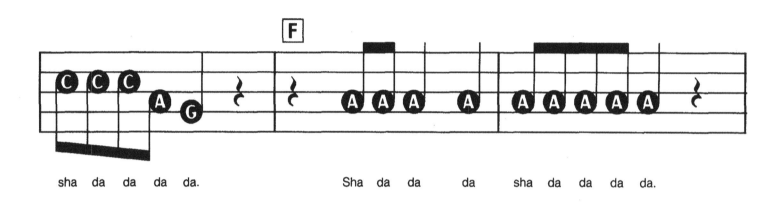

sha da da da da. Sha da da da sha da da da da.

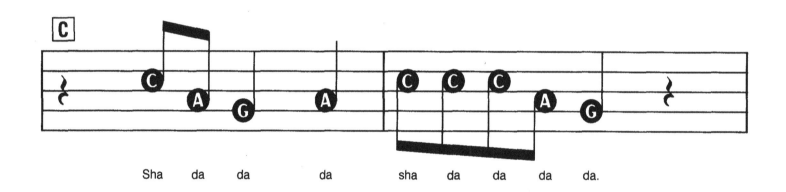

Sha da da da sha da da da da.

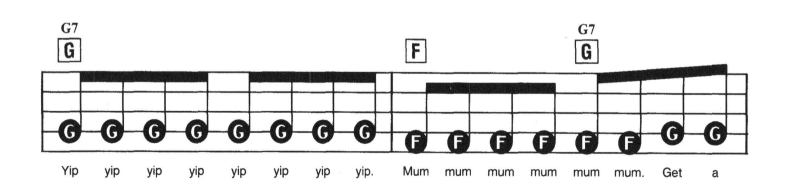

Yip yip yip yip yip yip yip yip. Mum mum mum mum mum mum. Get a

31

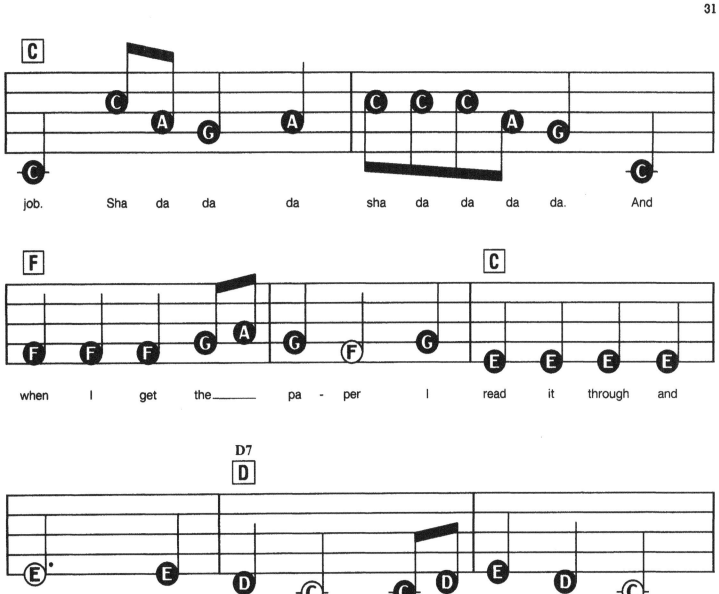

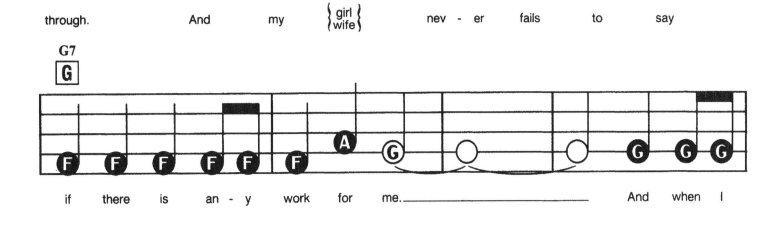

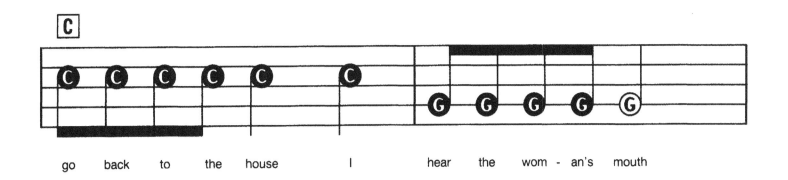

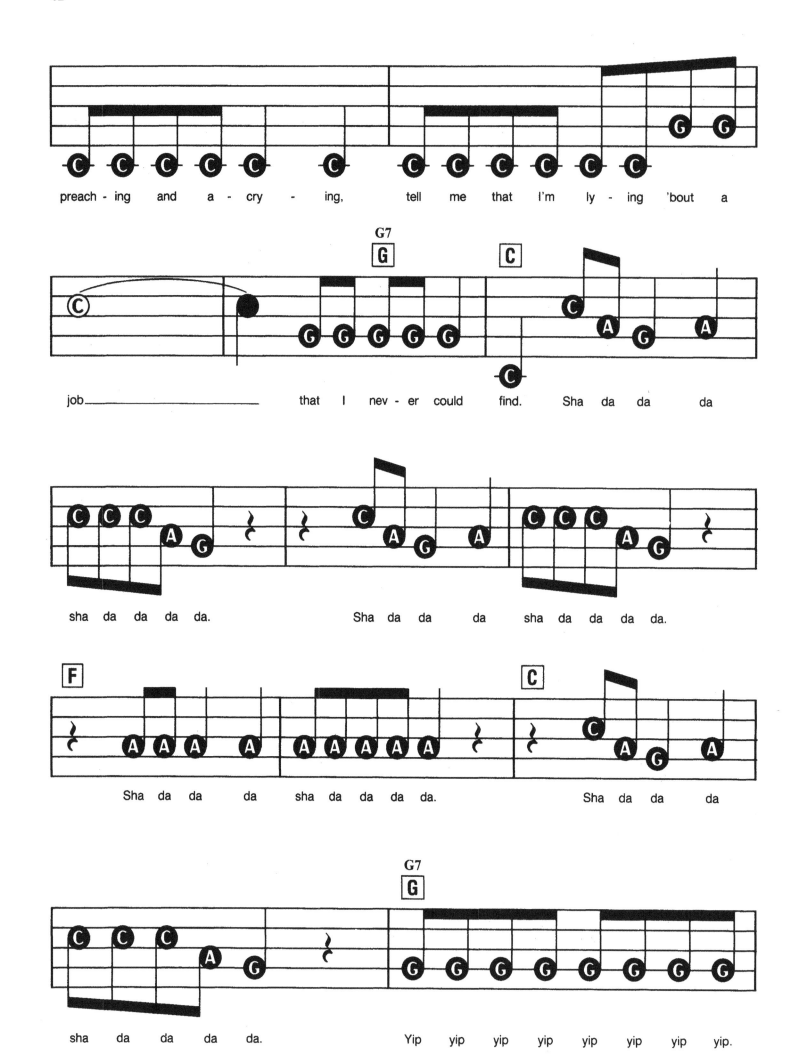

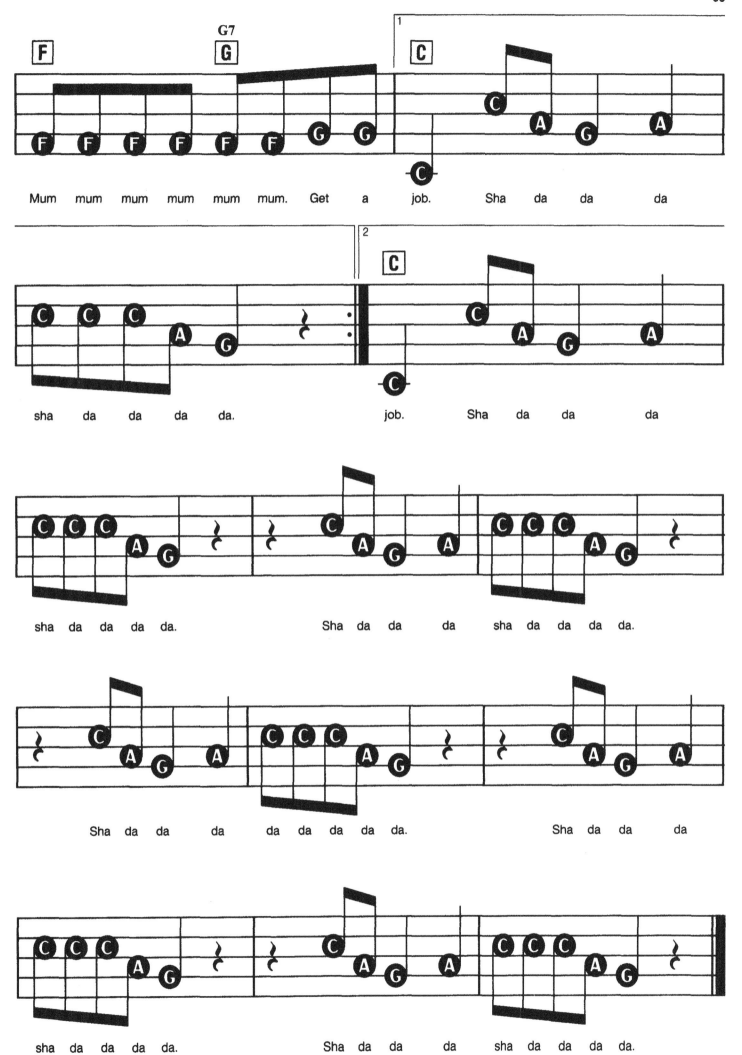

Good Vibrations

Registration 7
Rhythm: Rock

Words and Music by Brian Wilson
and Mike Love

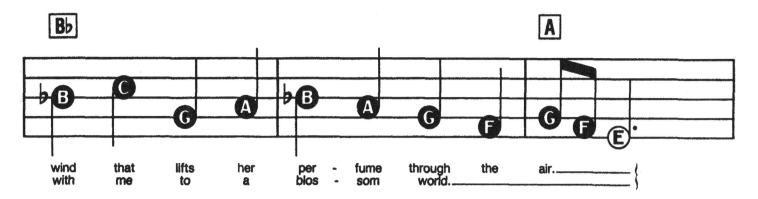

wind that lifts her per - fume through the air.\
with me to a blos - som world.

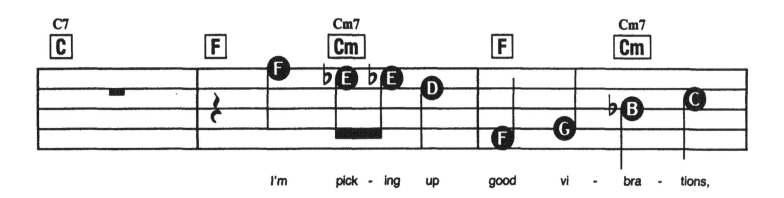

I'm pick - ing up good vi - bra - tions,

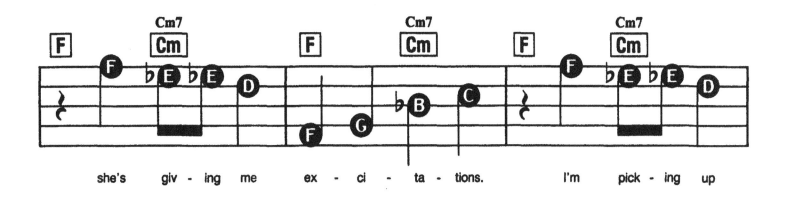

she's giv - ing me ex - ci - ta - tions. I'm pick - ing up

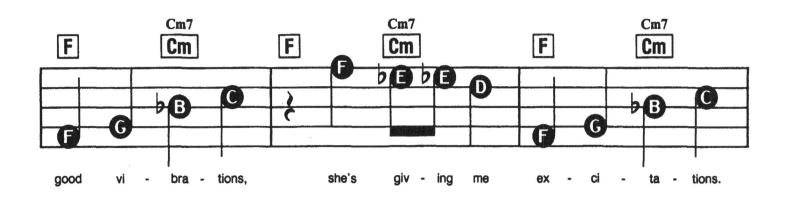

good vi - bra - tions, she's giv - ing me ex - ci - ta - tions.

36

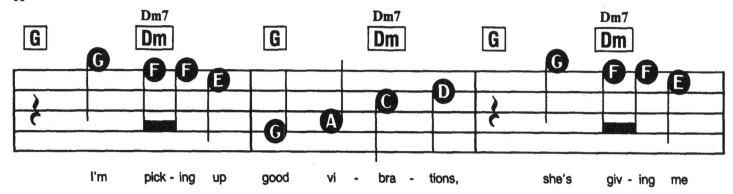

I'm pick - ing up good vi - bra - tions, she's giv - ing me

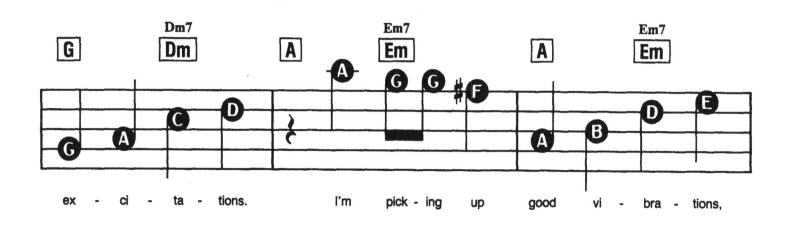

ex - ci - ta - tions. I'm pick - ing up good vi - bra - tions,

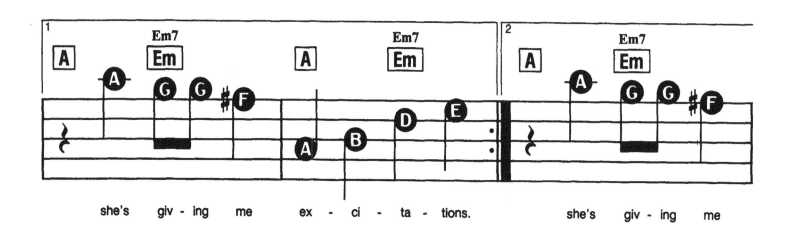

she's giv - ing me ex - ci - ta - tions. she's giv - ing me

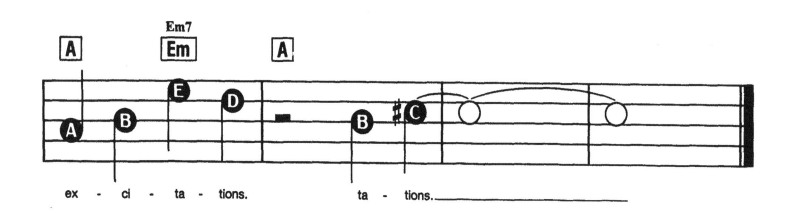

ex - ci - ta - tions. ta - tions._____

The Great Pretender

Registration 4
Rhythm: Fox Trot or Swing

Words and Music by
Buck Ram

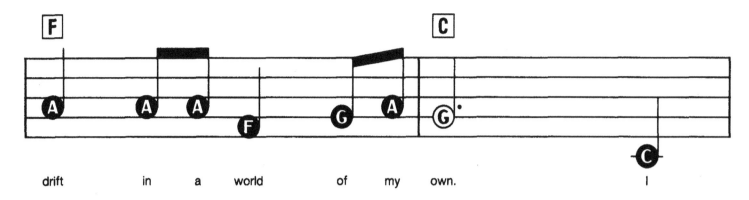

drift in a world of my own. I

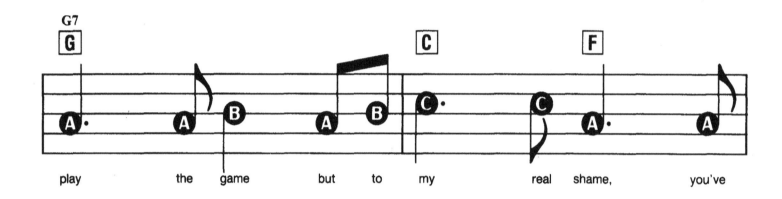

play the game but to my real shame, you've

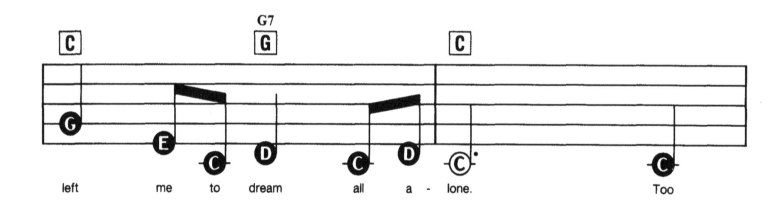

left me to dream all a - lone. Too

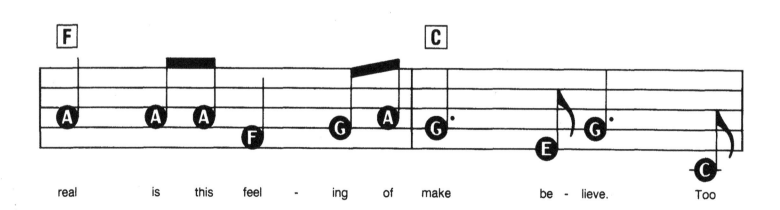

real is this feel - ing of make be - lieve. Too

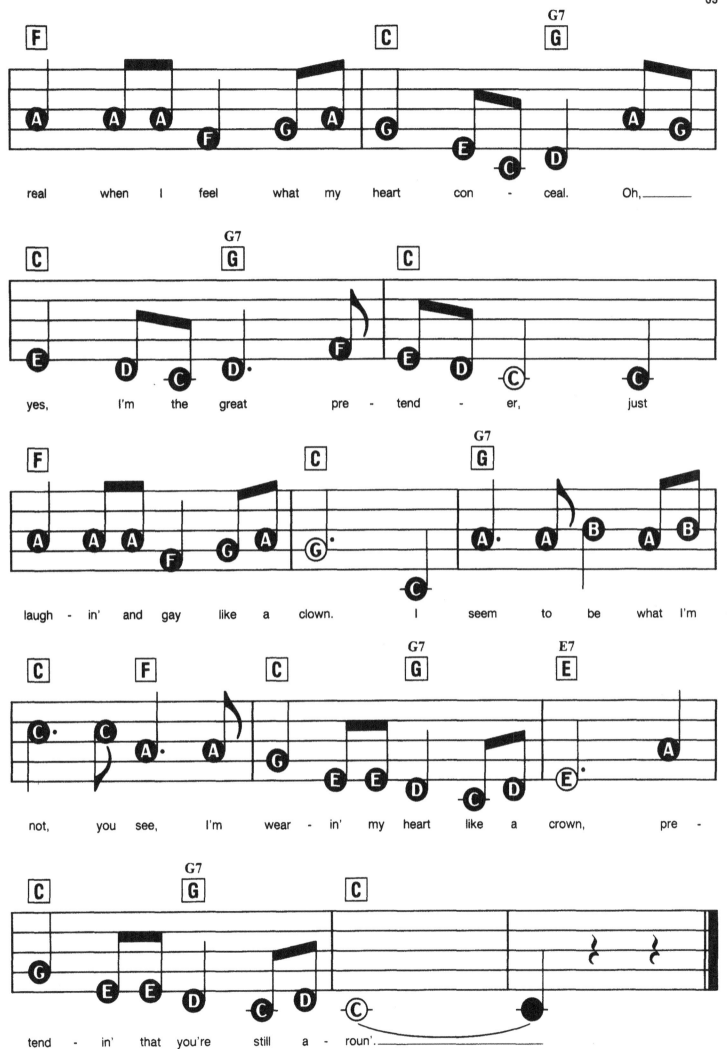

Green Onions

Registration 8
Rhythm: Swing

Written by Al Jackson, Jr.,
Lewis Steinberg, Booker T. Jones
and Steve Cropper

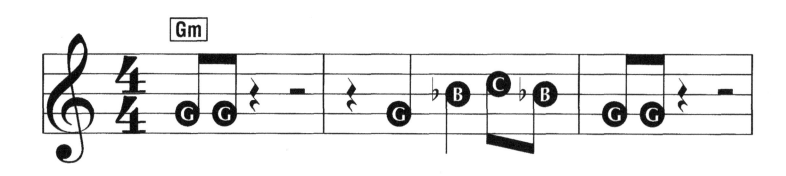

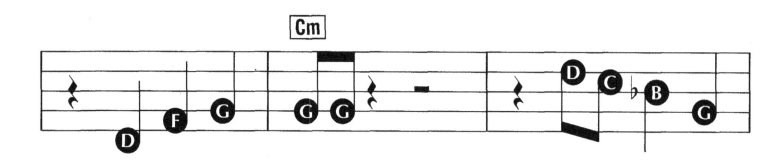

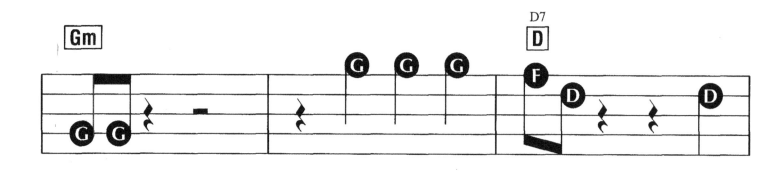

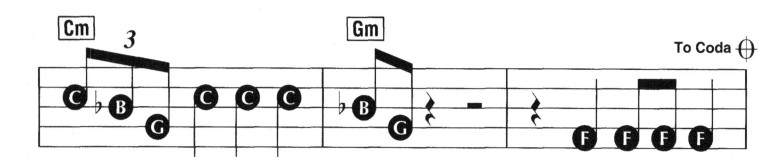

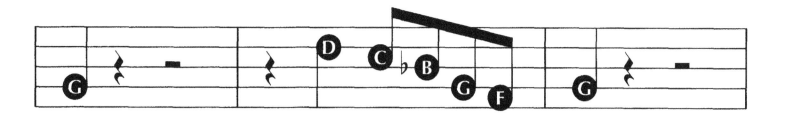

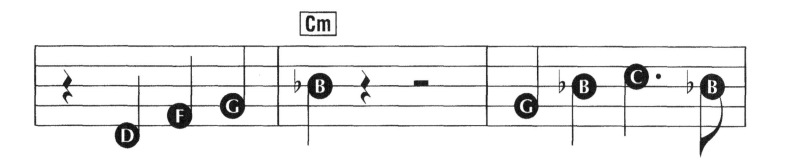

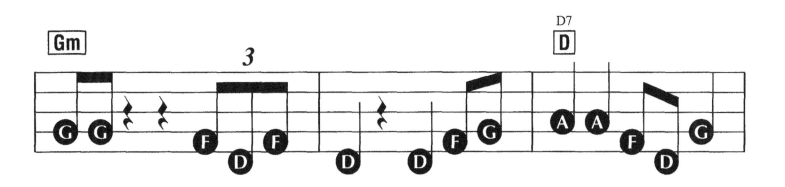

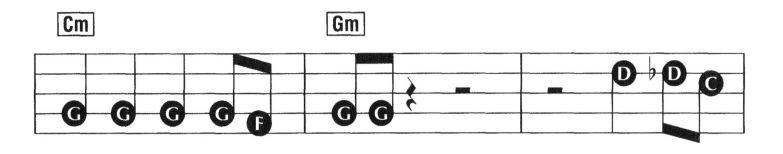

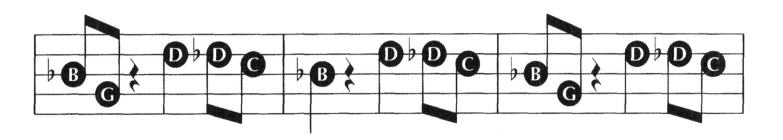

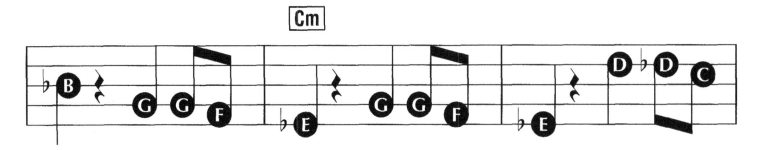

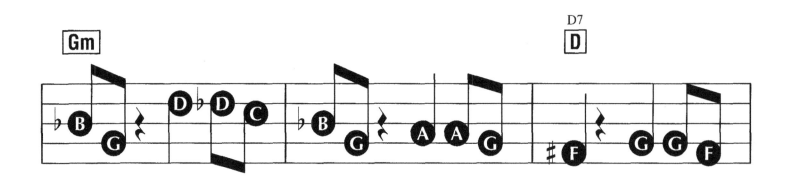

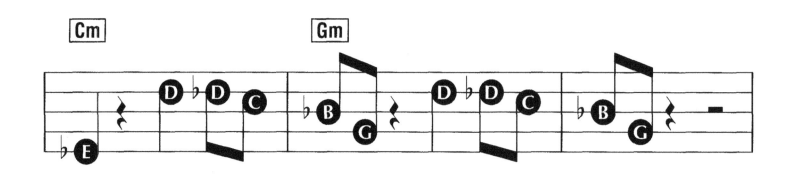

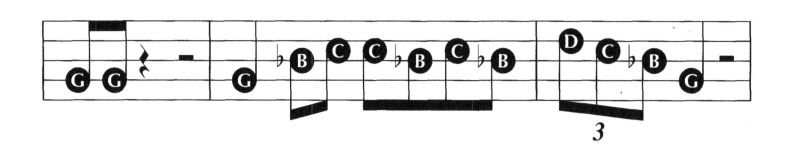

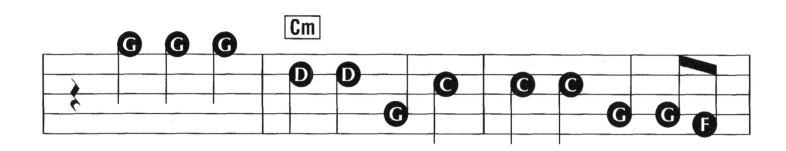

43

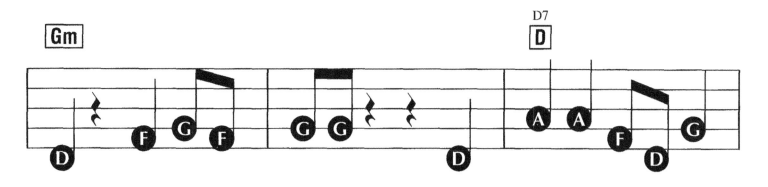

D.C. al Coda
(Return to beginning
Play to ⊕ and
Skip to Coda)

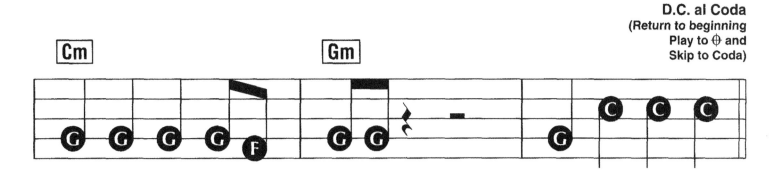

CODA

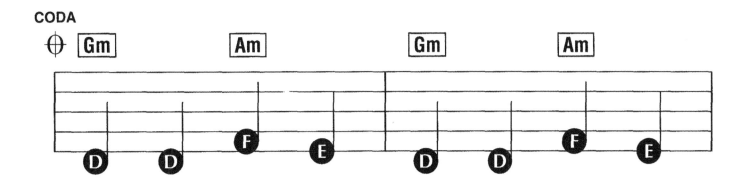

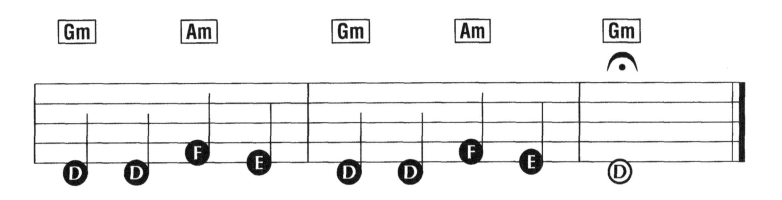

Heatwave
(Love Is Like a Heatwave)

Registration 4
Rhythm: Swing or Shuffle

Words and Music by Edward Holland,
Lamont Dozier and Brian Holland

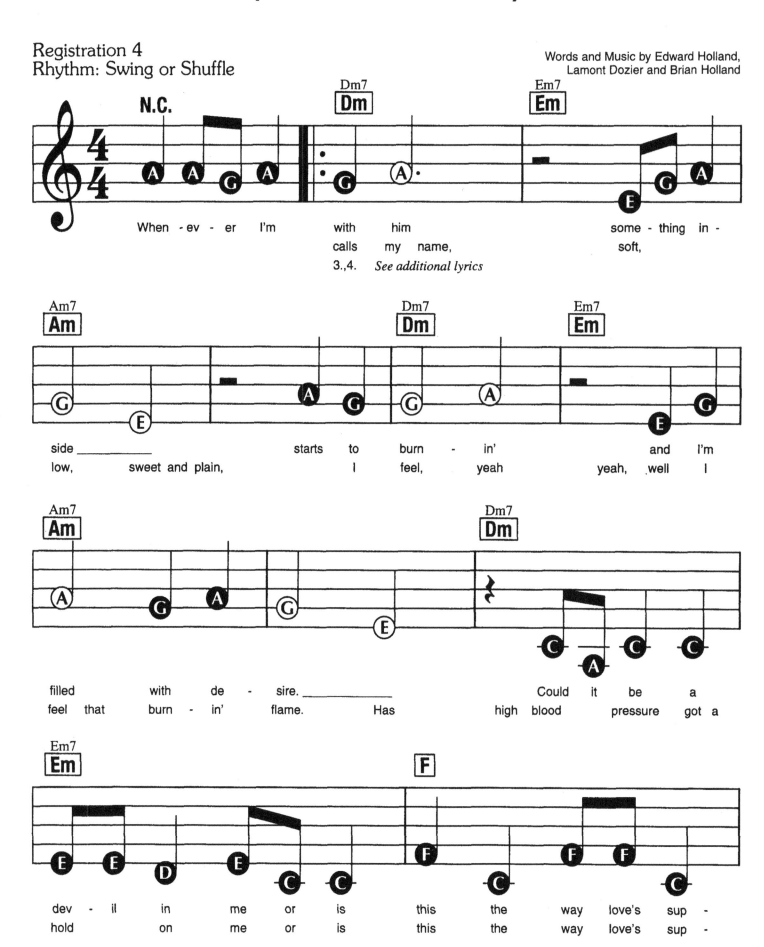

posed to be?
posed to be? } It's like a heat wave burn - in' in my

heart. _____ I can't keep from cry - in'.

It's tear - in' me a - part.

2. When - ev - er he
3. Some - times ____ I
4. Yeah yeah yeah

Additional Lyrics

3. Sometimes I stare into space,
   tears all over my face.
   I can't explain it,
   Don't understand it.
   I ain't never felt like this before.
   Now that funny feelin' has me amazed.
   I don't know what to do, my head's in a haze.

4. Yeah yeah yeah yeah yeah
   yeah whoa ho.
   Yeah yeah yeah yeah ho.
   Don't pass up this chance.
   This time it's a true romance.

I Think We're Alone Now

Registration 2
Rhythm: 8 Beat or Rock

Words and Music by
Ritchie Cordell

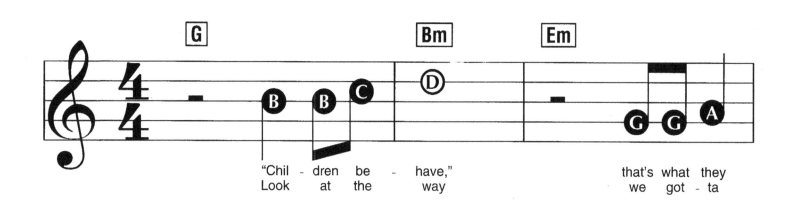

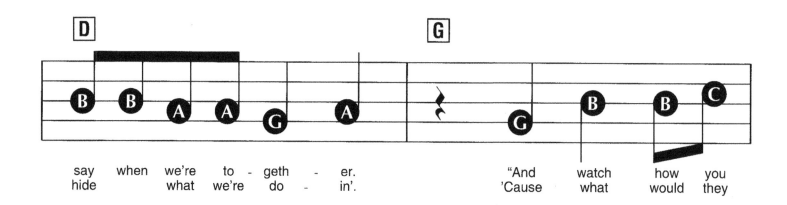

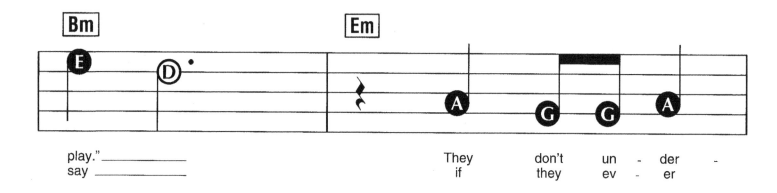

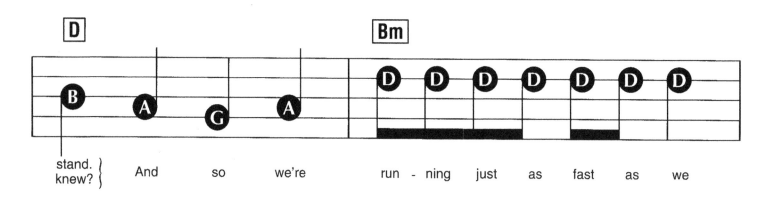

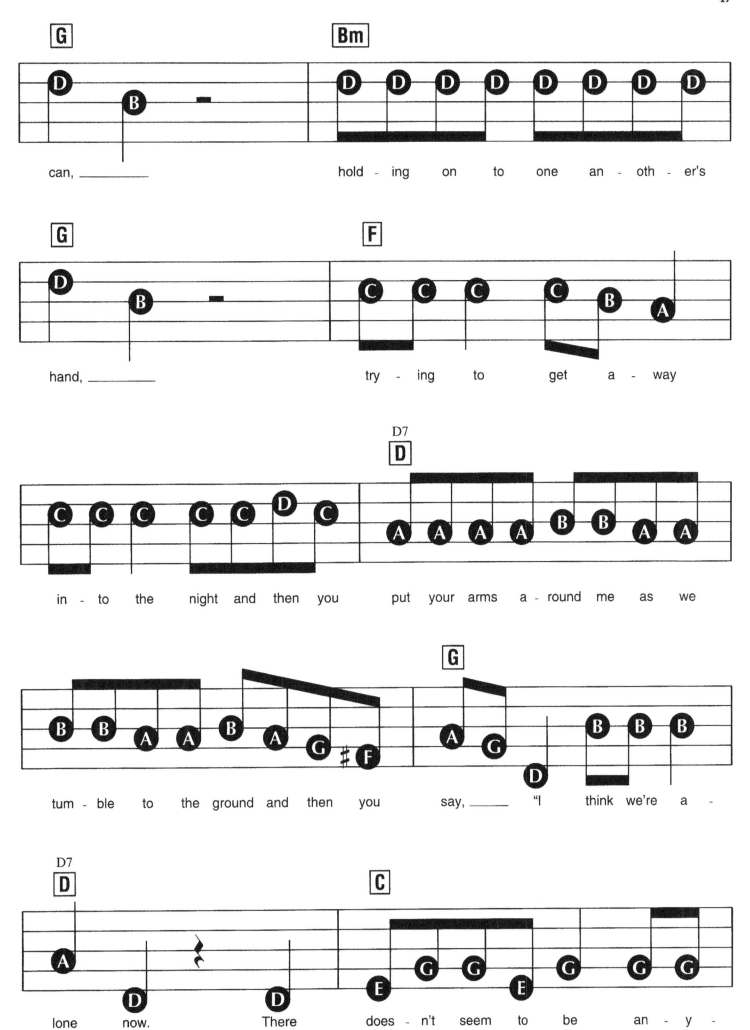

In the Midnight Hour

Registration 8
Rhythm: 8 Beat or Rock

Words and Music by Steve Cropper
and Wilson Pickett

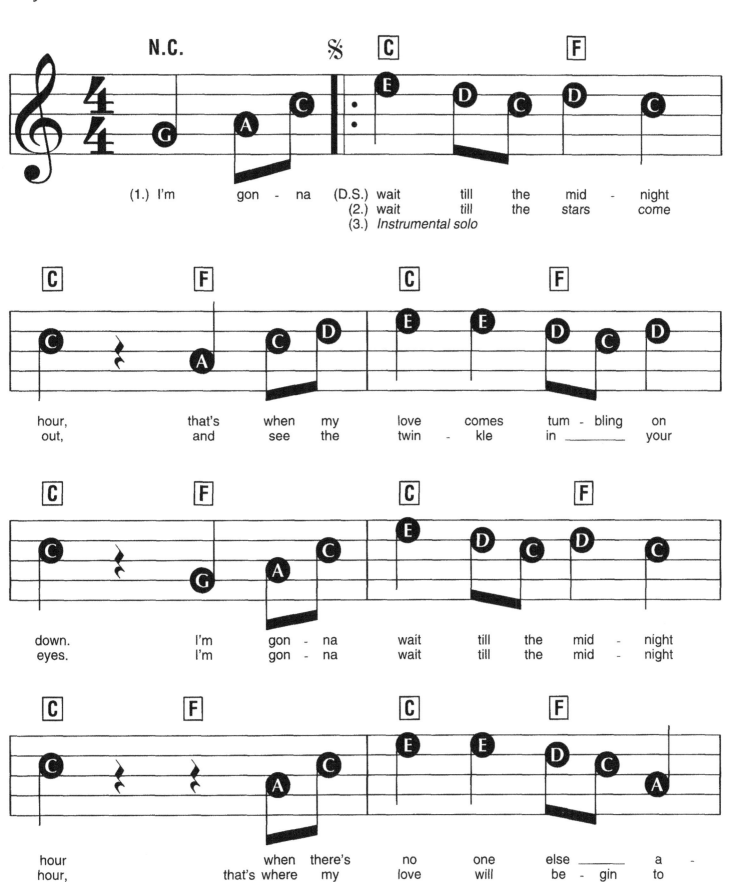

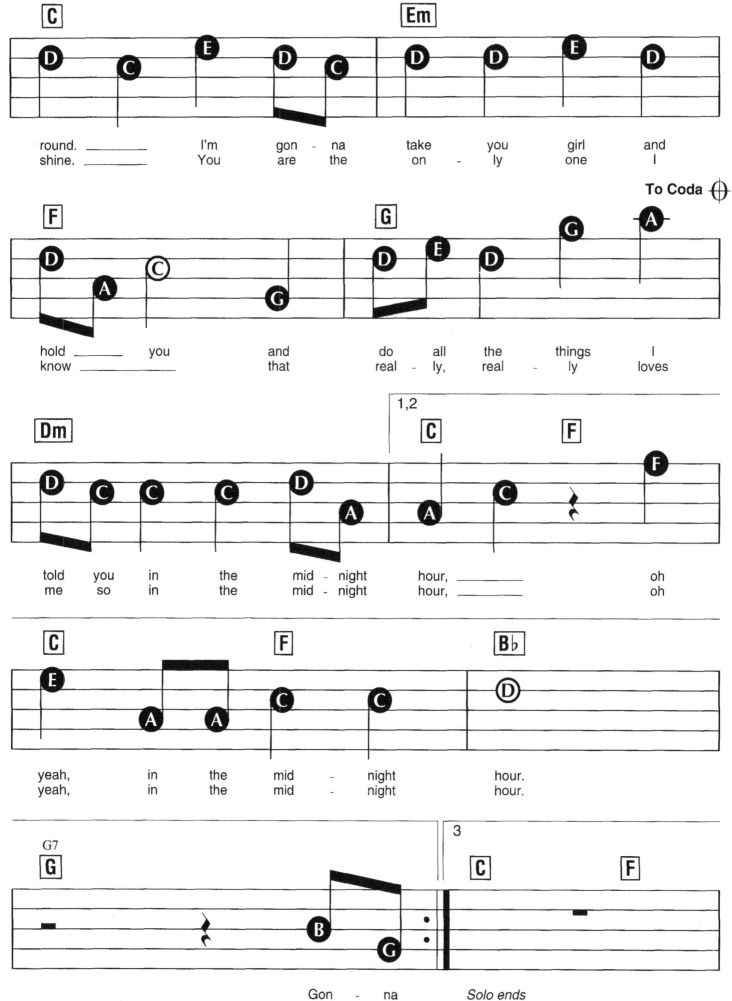

To Coda ⊕

round. _____ I'm gon - na take you girl and
shine. _____ You are the on - ly one I

hold _____ you and do all the things I
know _____ that real - ly, real - ly loves

1,2

told you in the mid - night hour, _____ oh
me so in the mid - night hour, _____ oh

yeah, in the mid - night hour.
yeah, in the mid - night hour.

3

G7

Gon - na *Solo ends*
Instrumental solo

51

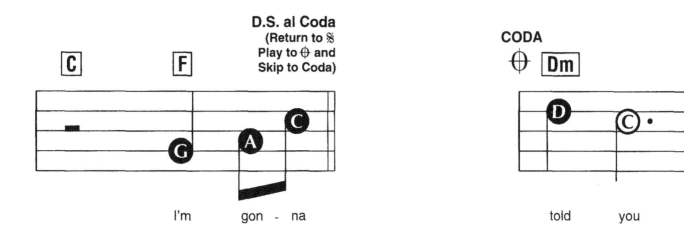

I'm   gon - na

CODA

told   you

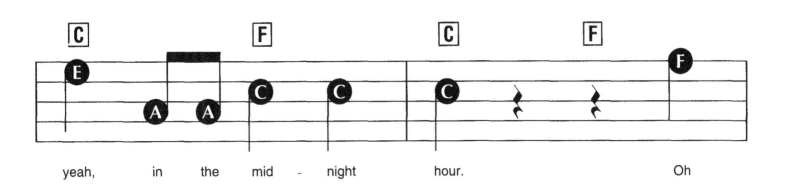

in   the   mid - night _____   hour,   oh

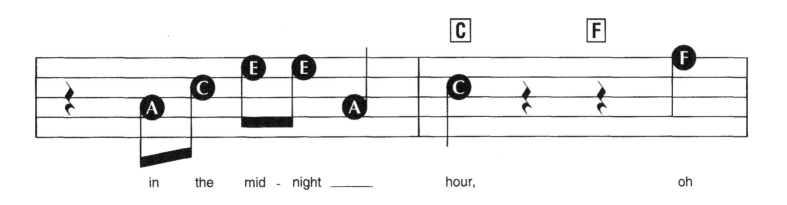

yeah,   in   the   mid - night   hour.   Oh

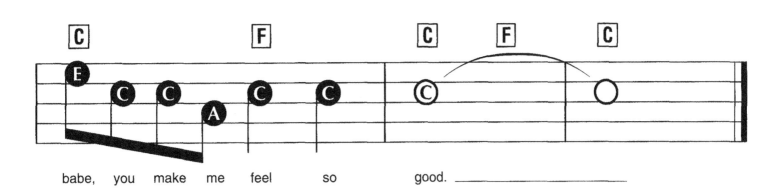

babe,   you   make   me   feel   so   good. _____

Indian Reservation

Registration 1
Rhythm: 8 Beat or Rock

Words and Music by
John D. Loudermilk

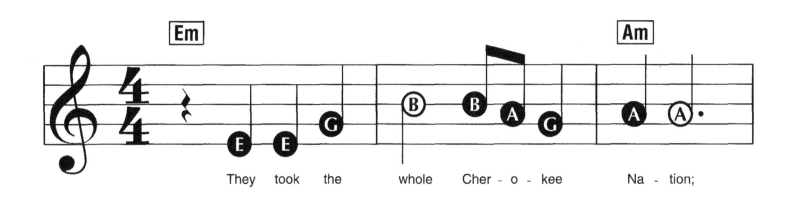

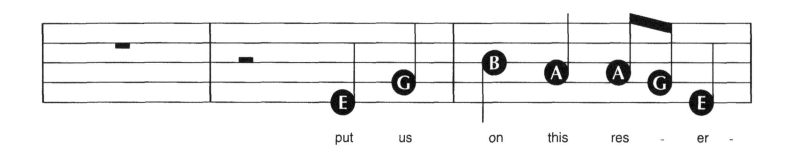

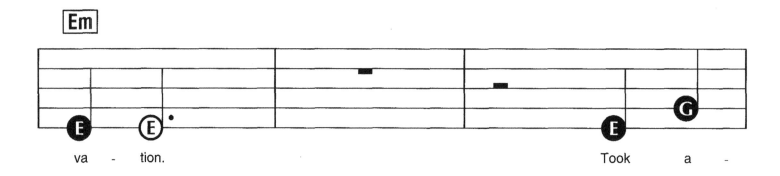

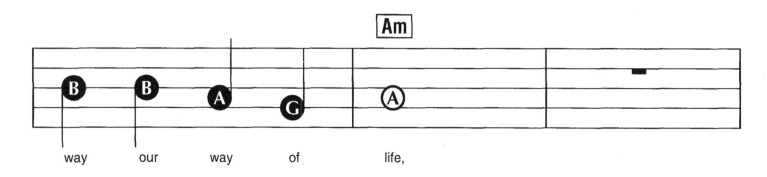

53

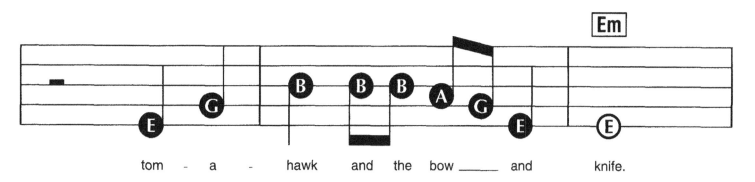

tom - a - hawk and the bow _____ and knife.

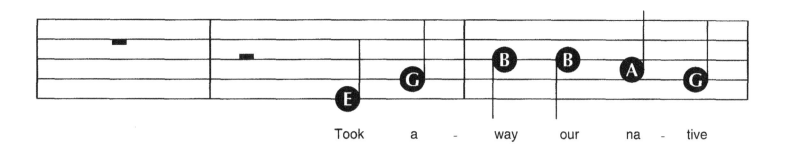

Took a - way our na - tive

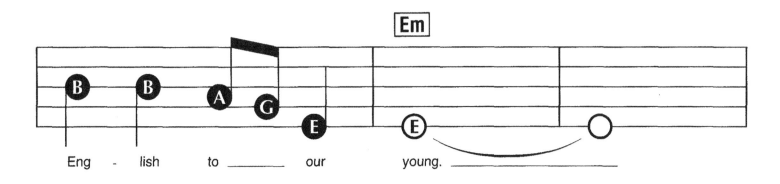

tongue, taught their

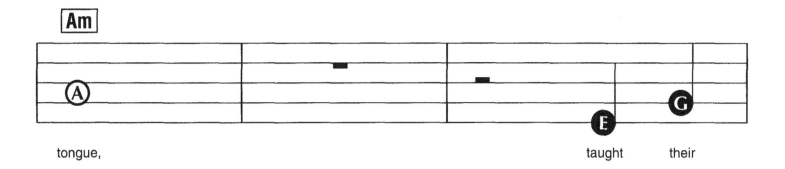

Eng - lish to _____ our young. _____

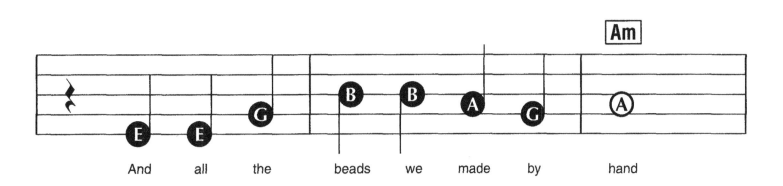

And all the beads we made by hand

54

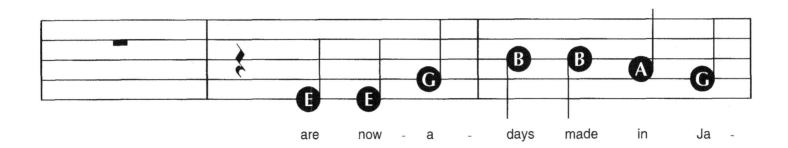

are   now - a - days   made   in   Ja -

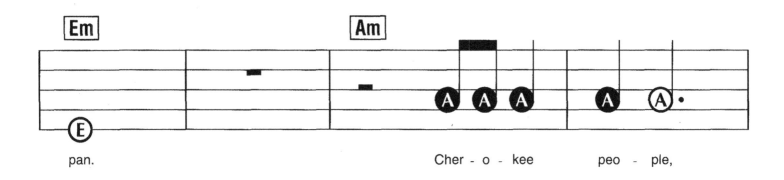

pan.   Cher - o - kee   peo - ple,

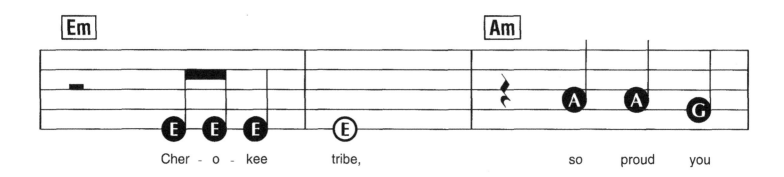

Cher - o - kee   tribe,   so   proud   you

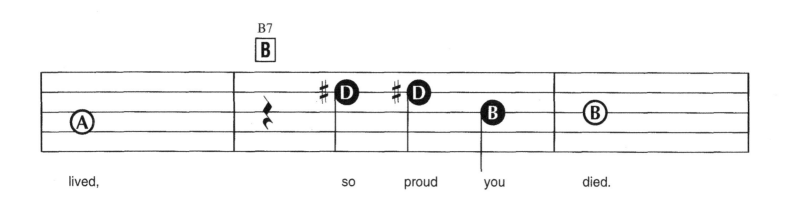

lived,   so   proud   you   died.

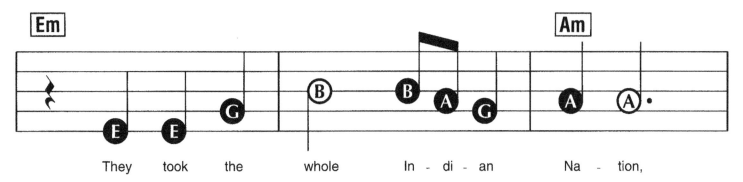

They took the whole In - di - an Na - tion,

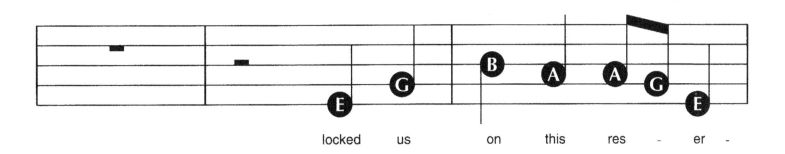

locked us on this res - er -

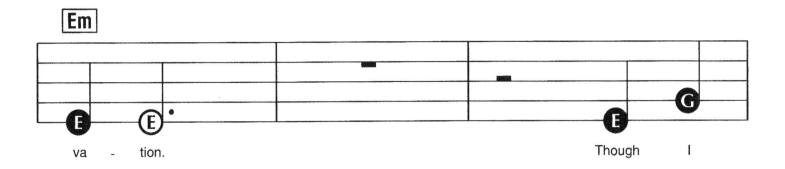

va - tion. Though I

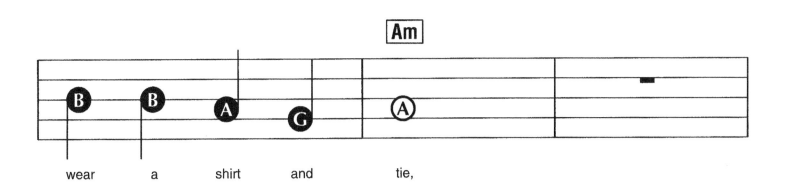

wear a shirt and tie,

56

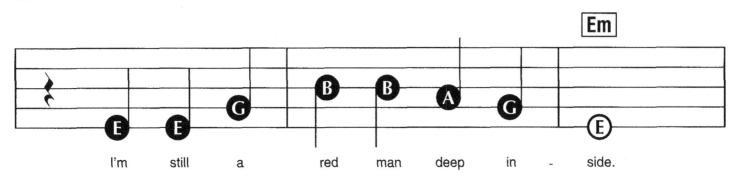

I'm still a red man deep in - side.

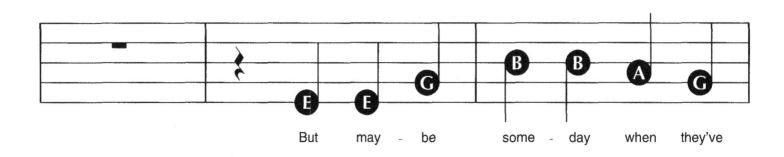

But may - be some - day when they've

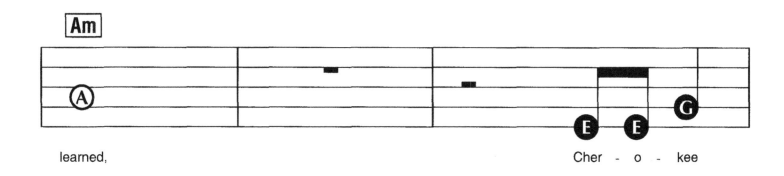

learned, Cher - o - kee

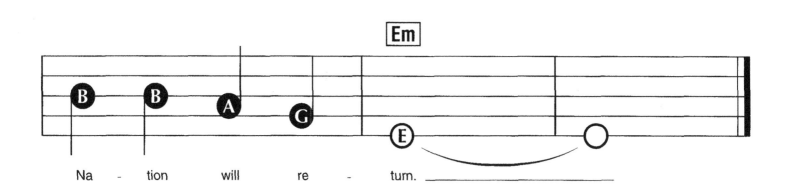

Na - tion will re - turn. _____

La Bamba

Registration 4
Rhythm: Latin

By Ritchie Valens

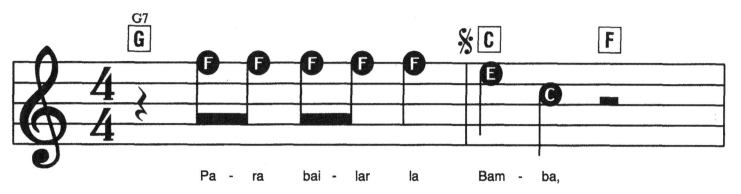

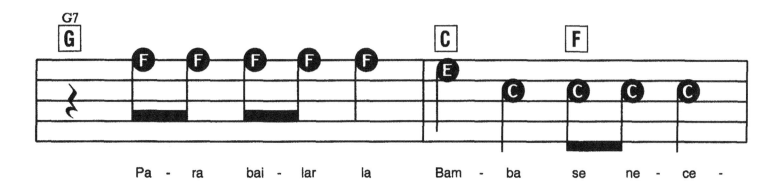

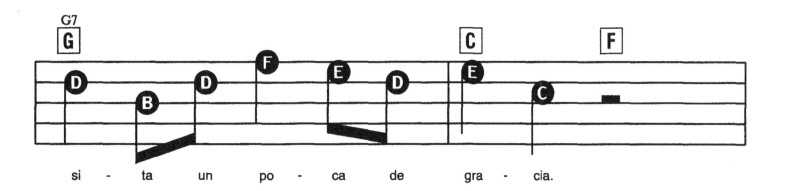

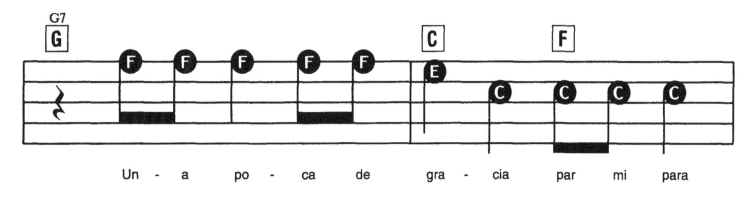

58

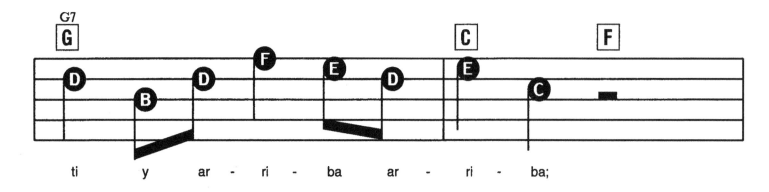

ti y ar - ri - ba ar - ri - ba;

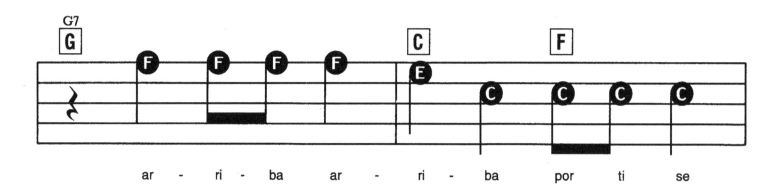

ar - ri - ba ar - ri - ba por ti se

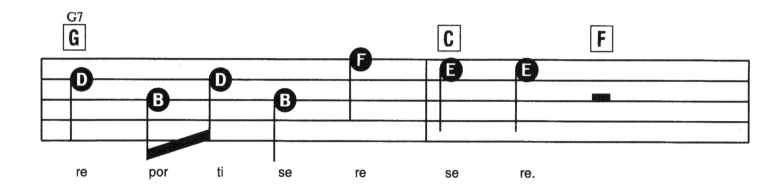

re por ti se re se re.

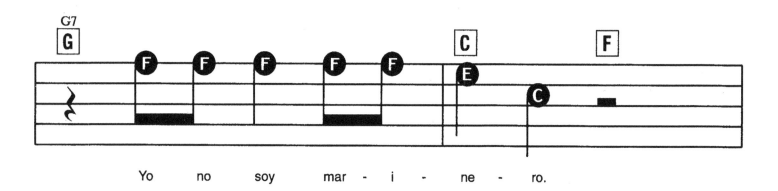

Yo no soy mar - i - ne - ro.

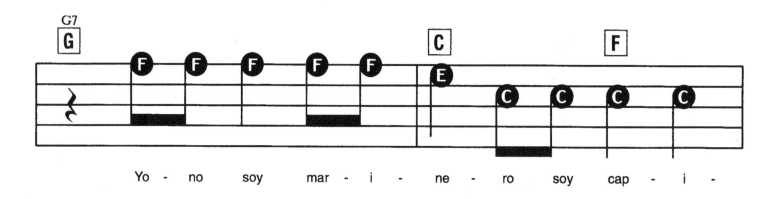

Yo - no soy mar - i - ne - ro soy cap - i -

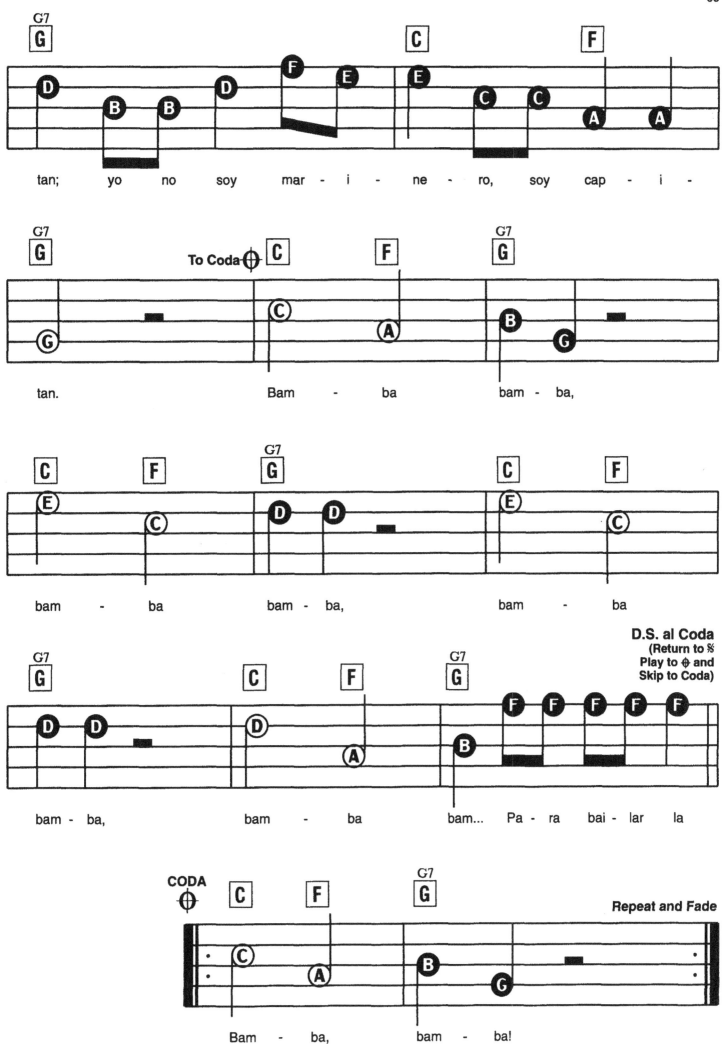

Last Date

Registration 8
Rhythm: Slow Rock or Country Swing

By Floyd Cramer

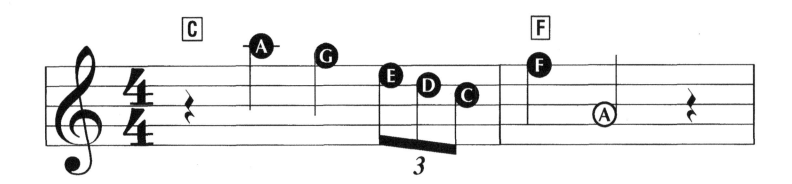

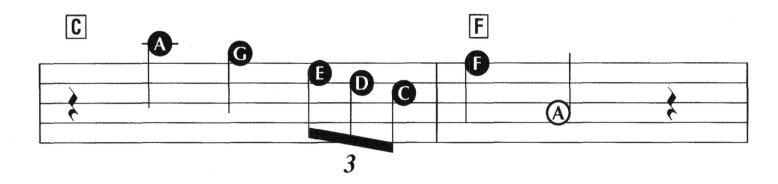

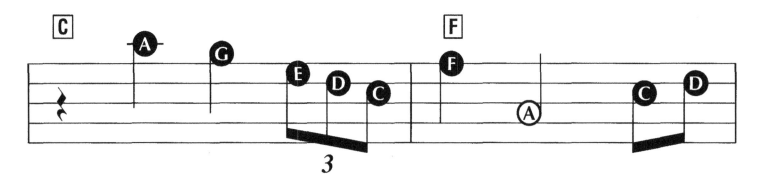

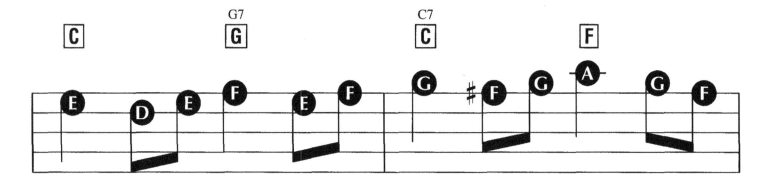

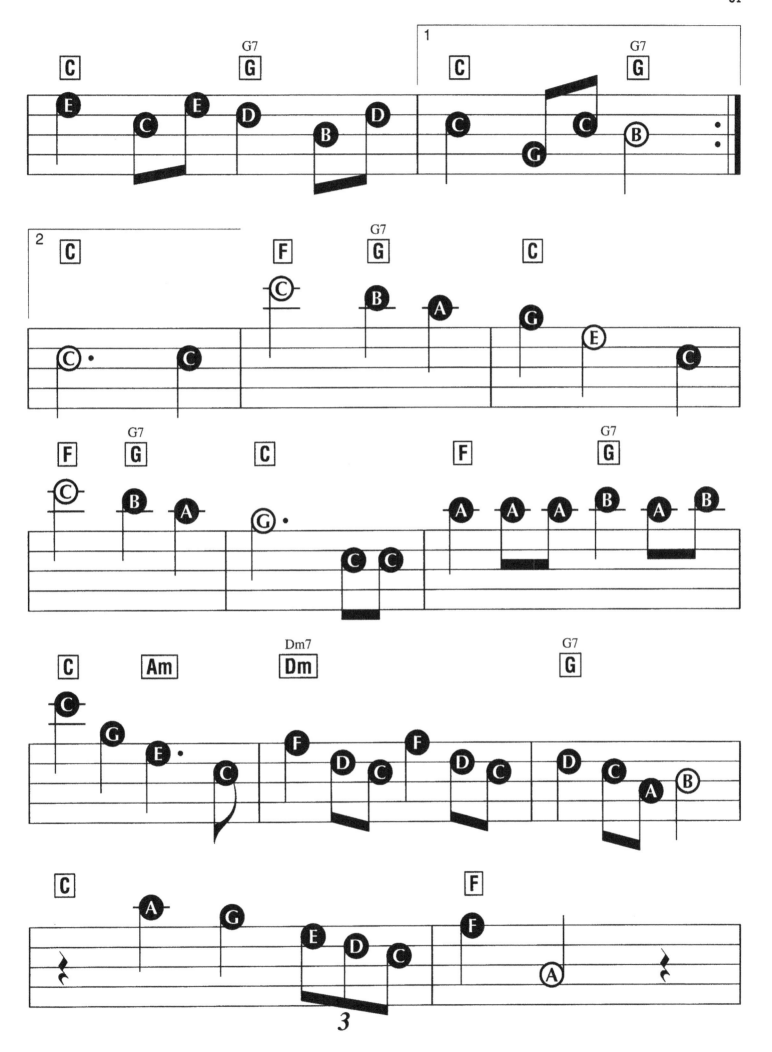

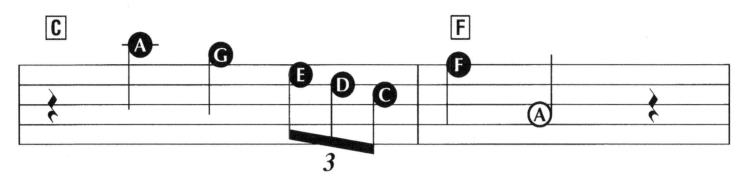

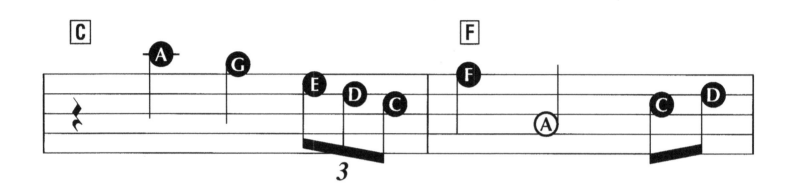

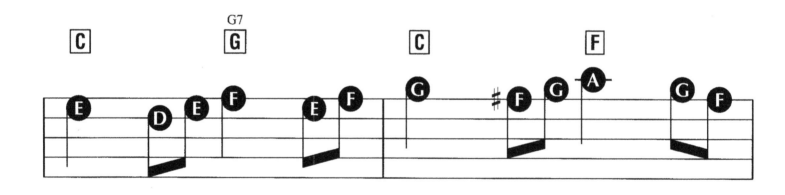

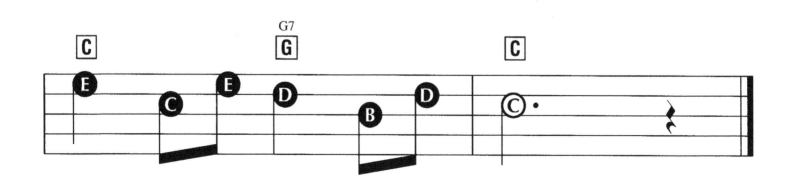

Let's Get Together

Registration 7
Rhythm: 8 Beat or Rock

Words and Music by
Chet Powers

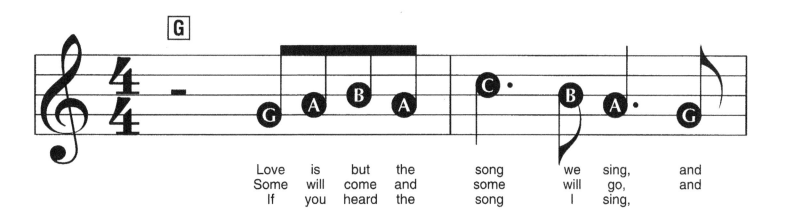

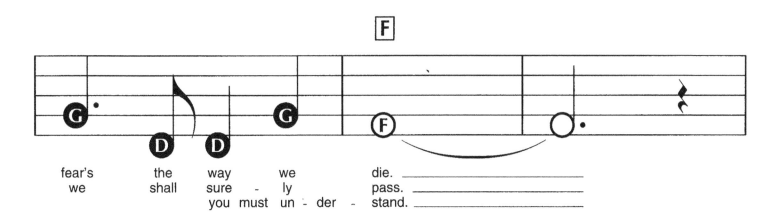

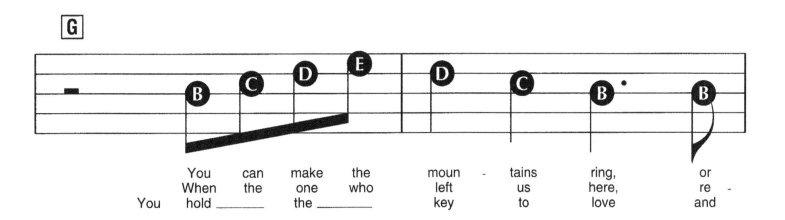

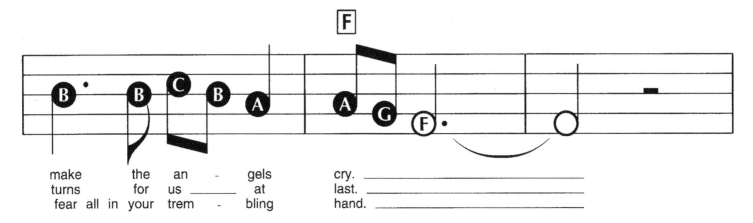

make   the an - gels   cry. _____
turns   for us _____ at   last. _____
fear all in your trem - bling   hand. _____

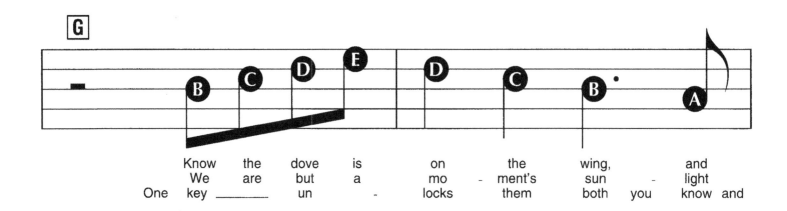

Know   the dove   is   on   the   wing,   and
We   are but a   mo -   ment's   sun -   light
One key _____ un   -   locks   them   both   you   know   and

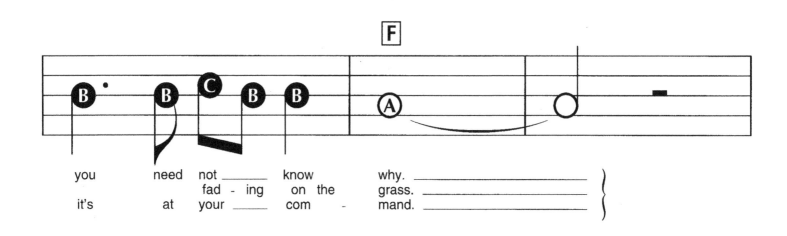

you   need not _____ know   why. _____
          fad - ing   on the   grass. _____
it's   at your _____ com -   mand. _____

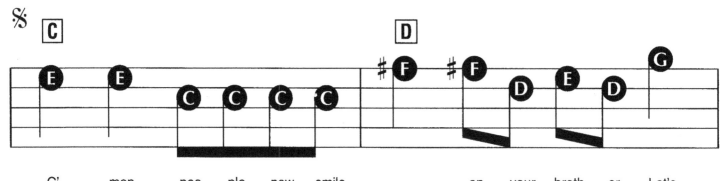

C' - mon peo - ple now smile _____ on your broth - er. Let's _____

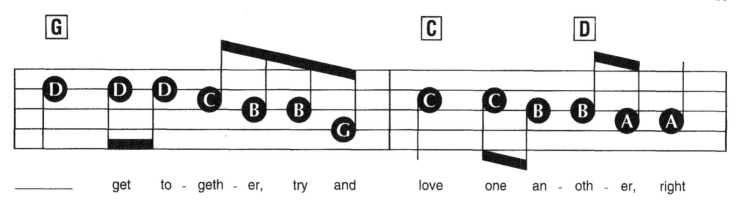

get to - geth - er, try and love one an - oth - er, right

To Coda

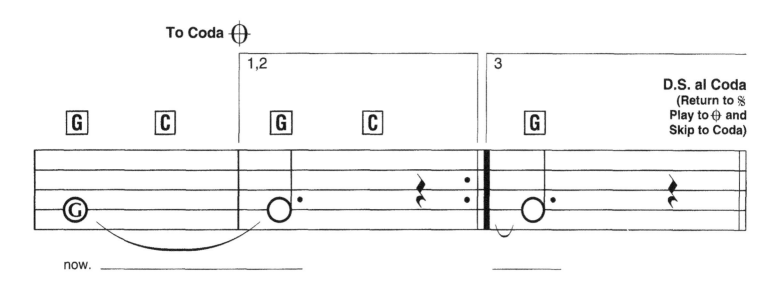

now.

Right now! Right now!

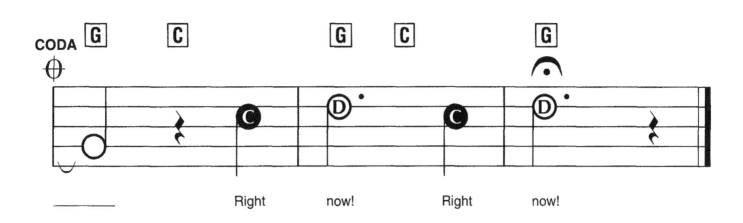

Let's Hang On

Registration 4
Rhythm: Rock or 8 Beat

Words and Music by Bob Crewe,
Denny Randell and Sandy Linzer

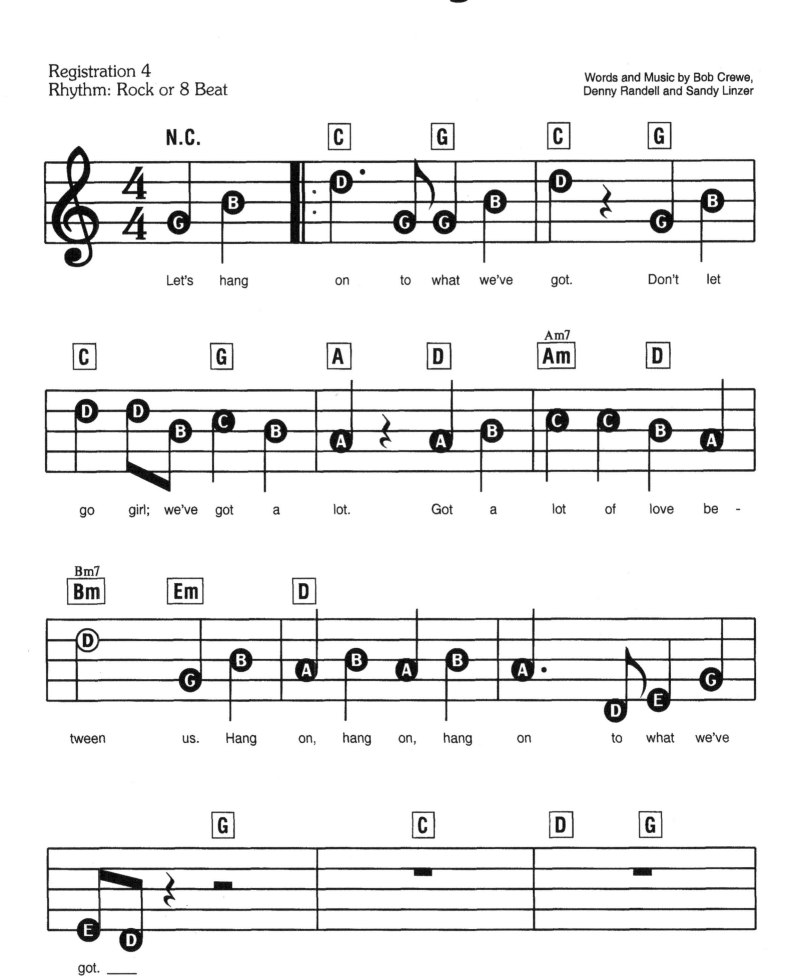

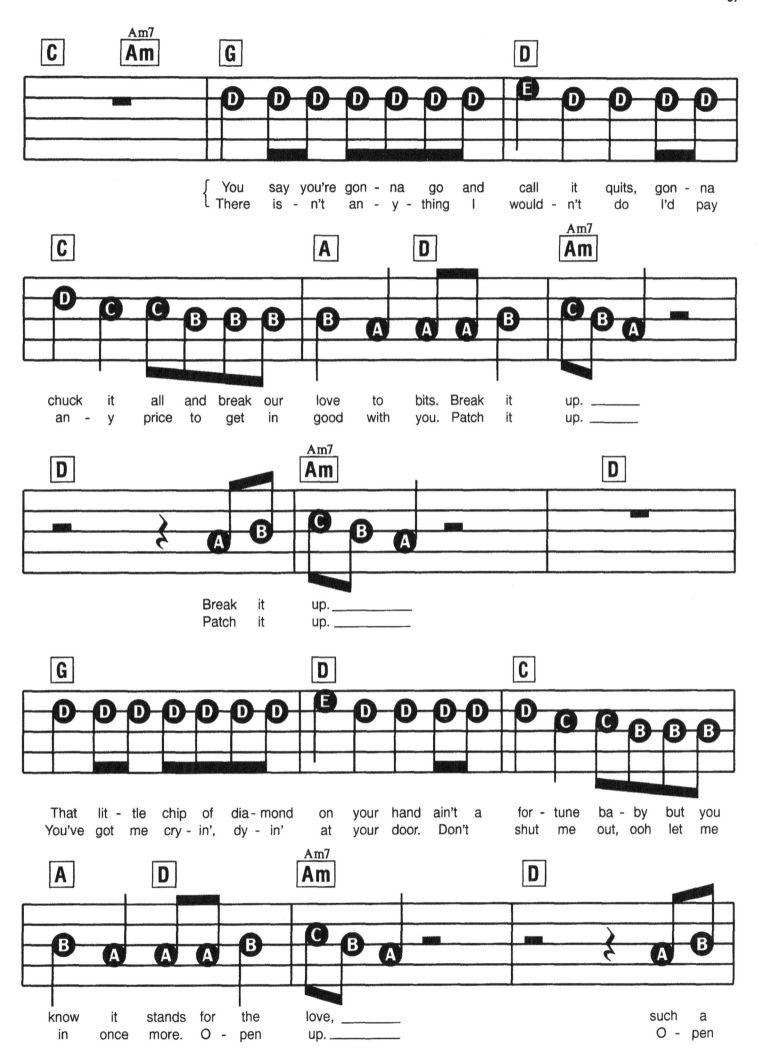

68

Mony, Mony

Registration 8
Rhythm: Rock

Words and Music by Bobby Bloom, Tommy James,
Ritchie Cordell and Bo Gentry

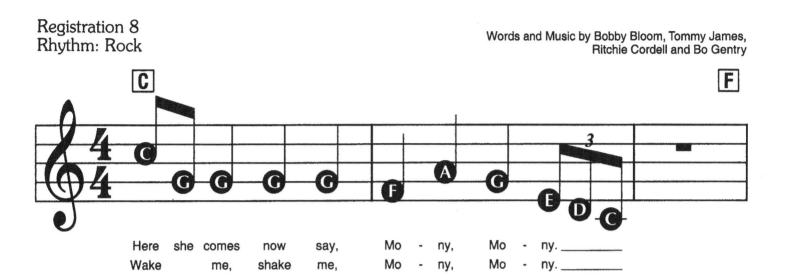

Here she comes now say, Mo - ny, Mo - ny. _____
Wake me, shake me, Mo - ny, Mo - ny. _____

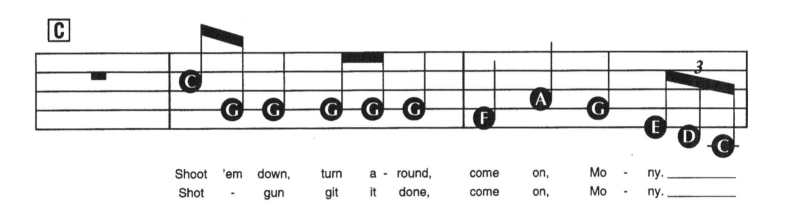

Shoot 'em down, turn a - round, come on, Mo - ny. _____
Shot - gun git it done, come on, Mo - ny. _____

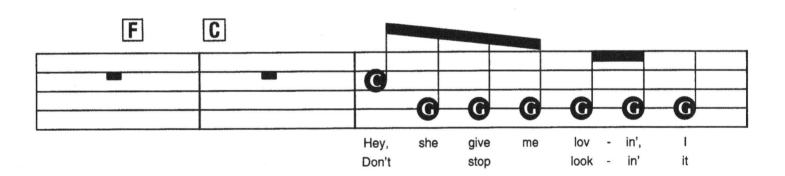

Hey, she give me lov - in', I
Don't stop look - in' it

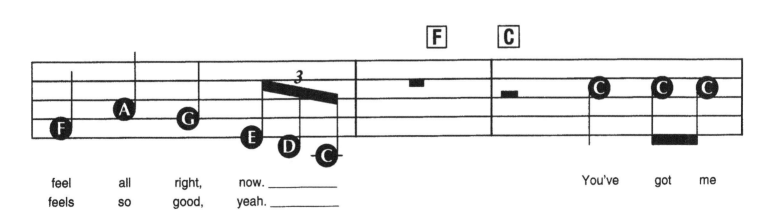

feel all right, now. _____
feels so good, yeah. _____

You've got me

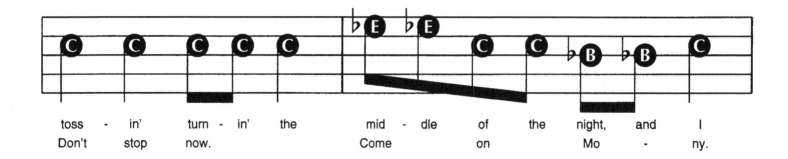

toss - in'   turn - in'   the   mid - dle   of   the   night,   and   I
Don't   stop   now.   Come   on   Mo   -   ny.

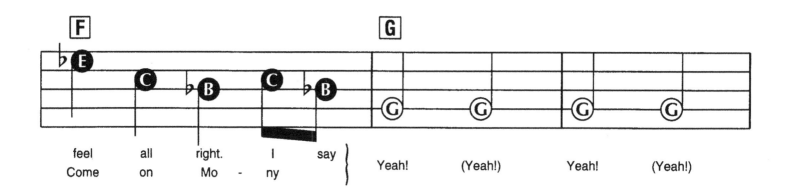

feel   all   right.   I   say   Yeah!   (Yeah!)   Yeah!   (Yeah!)
Come   on   Mo   -   ny

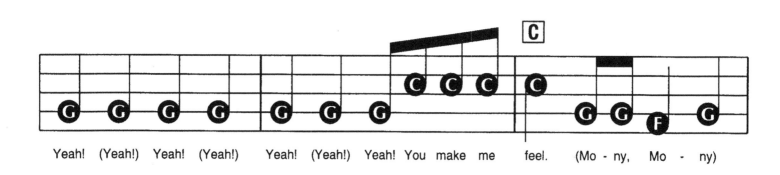

Yeah!   (Yeah!)   Yeah!   (Yeah!)   Yeah!   (Yeah!)   Yeah!   You   make   me   feel.   (Mo - ny,   Mo - ny)

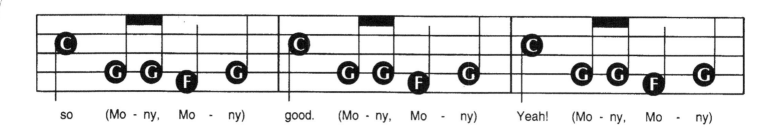

so   (Mo - ny,   Mo - ny)   good.   (Mo - ny,   Mo - ny)   Yeah!   (Mo - ny,   Mo - ny)

71

Yeah! (Mo - ny, Mo - ny) Yeah! (Mo - ny, Mo - ny) Yeah! (Mo - ny, Mo - ny)

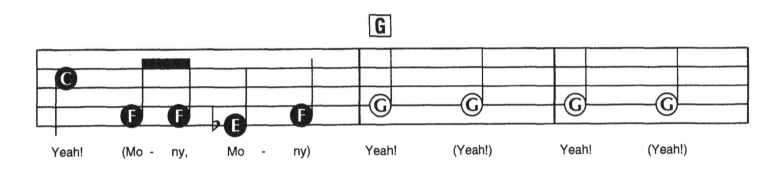

Yeah! (Mo - ny, Mo - ny) Yeah! (Yeah!) Yeah! (Yeah!)

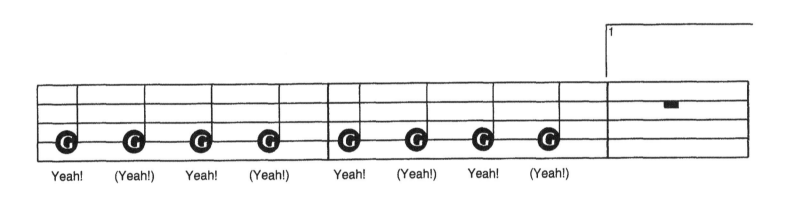

Yeah! (Yeah!) Yeah! (Yeah!) Yeah! (Yeah!) Yeah! (Yeah!)

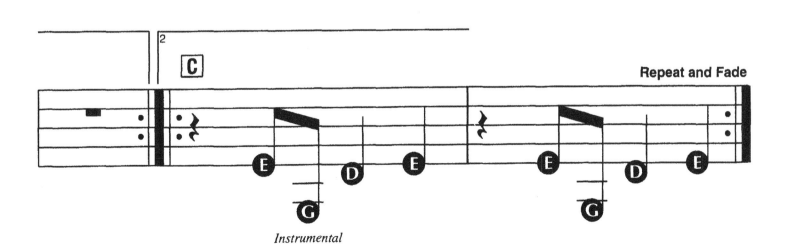

Repeat and Fade

Instrumental

Mellow Yellow

Registration 1
Rhythm: 8 Beat or Rock

Words and Music by
Donovan Leitch

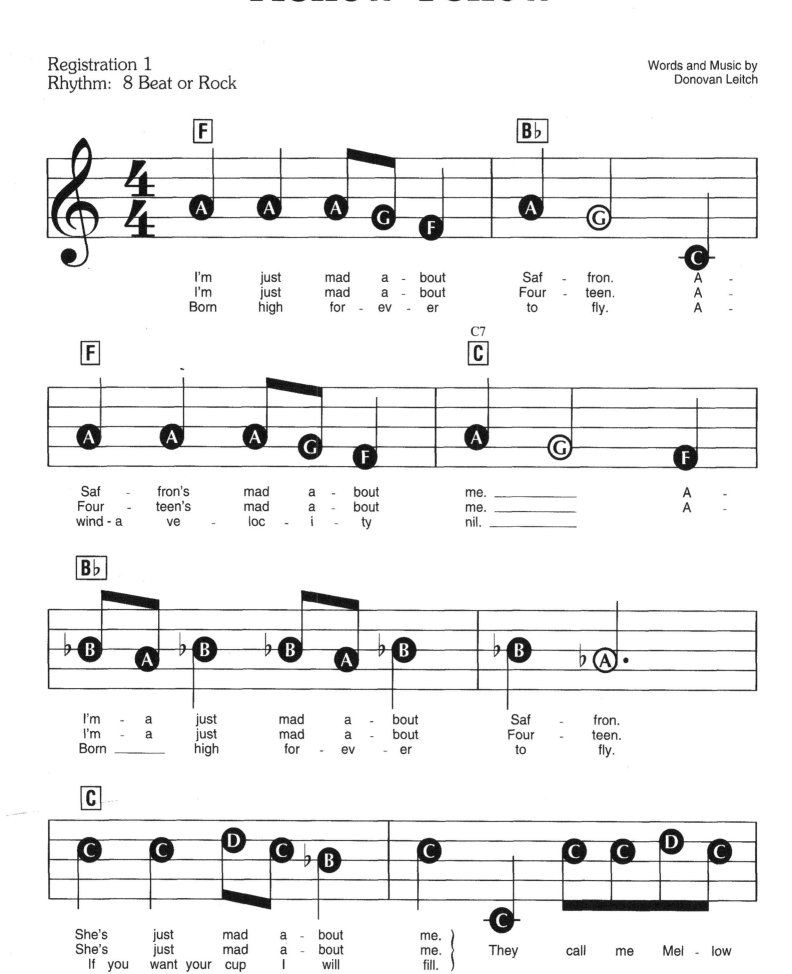

73

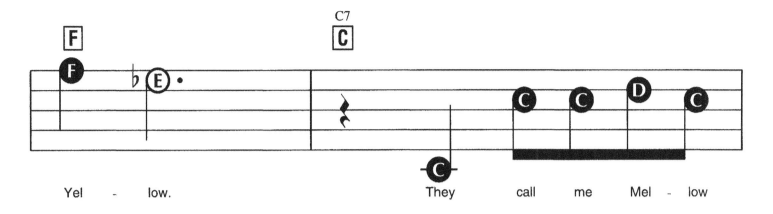

Yel - low.   They call me Mel - low

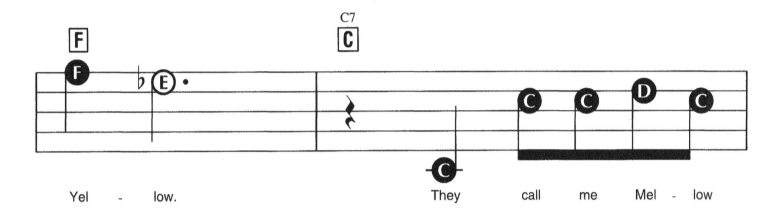

Yel - low.   They call me Mel - low

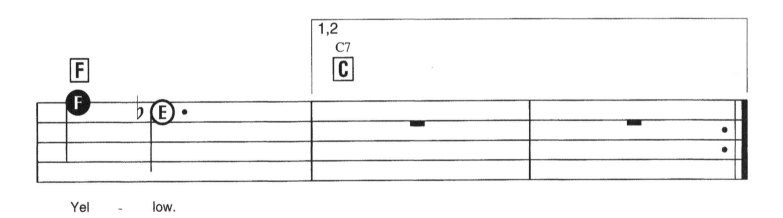

Yel - low.

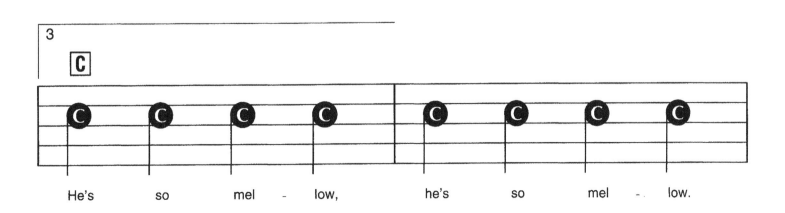

He's so mel - low,   he's so mel - low.

74

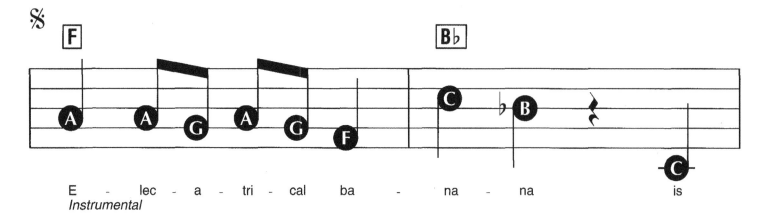

E - lec - a - tri - cal ba - na - na is

Instrumental

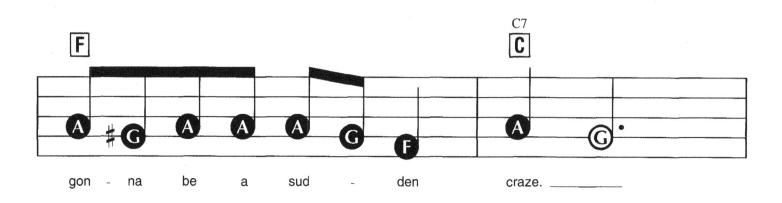

gon - na be a sud - den craze. _____

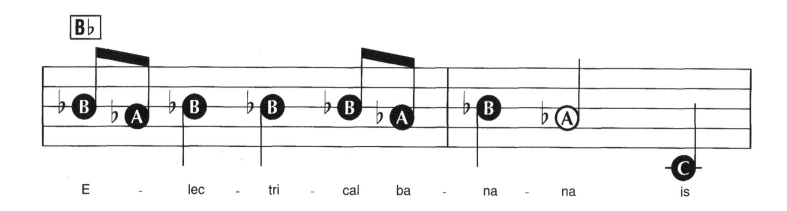

E - lec - tri - cal ba - na - na is

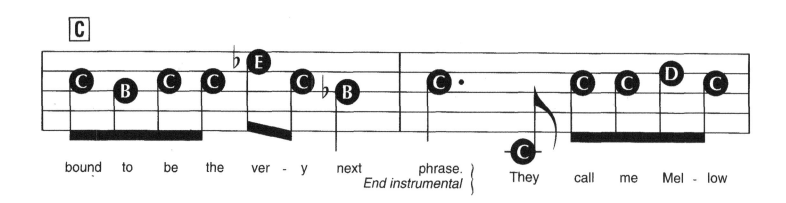

bound to be the ver - y next phrase.

End instrumental They call me Mel - low

75

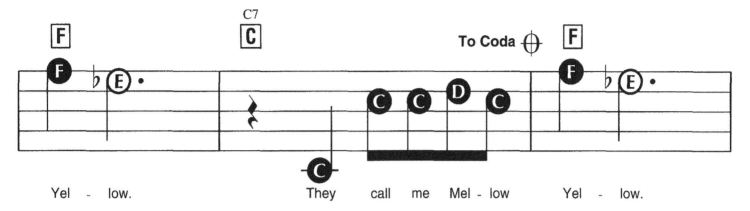

Yel - low.   They   call   me   Mel - low   Yel - low.

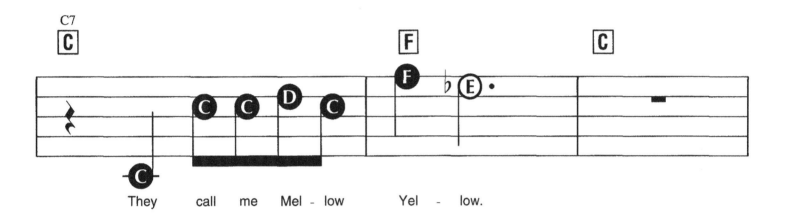

They   call   me   Mel - low   Yel - low.

D.S. al Coda
(Return to %
Play to ⊕ and
Skip to Coda)

CODA

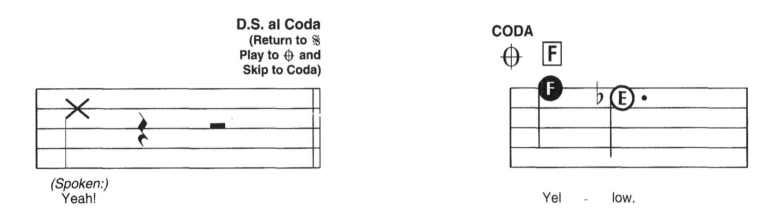

(Spoken:)
Yeah!

Yel - low.

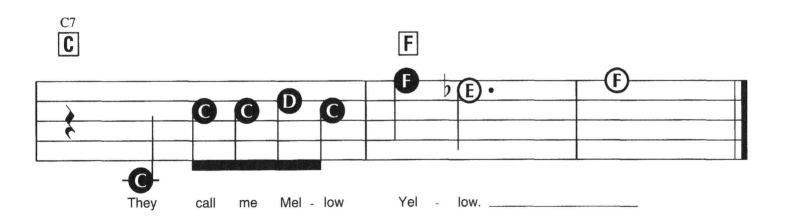

They   call   me   Mel - low   Yel - low. _____

My Girl

Registration 4
Rhythm: Rock or 8 Beat

Words and Music by William "Smokey" Robinson
and Ronald White

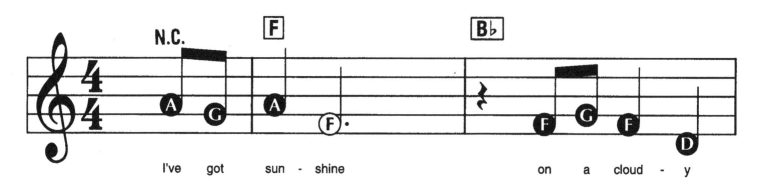

I've got sun - shine on a cloud - y

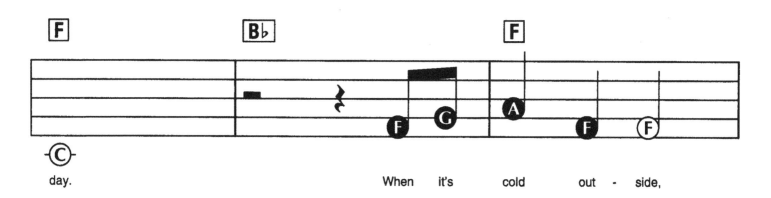

day. When it's cold out - side,

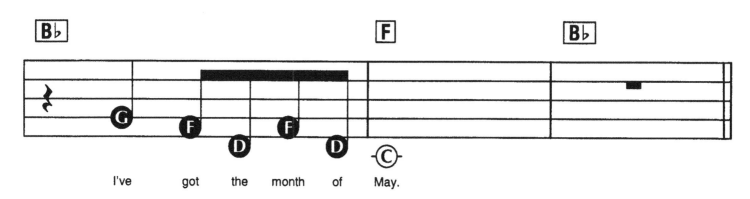

I've got the month of May.

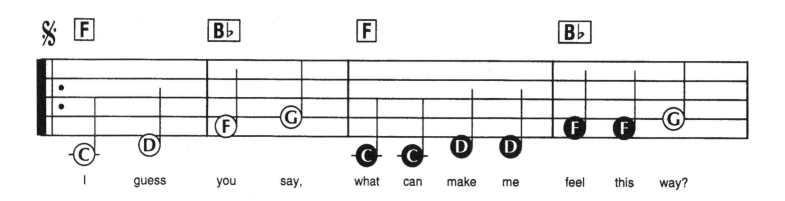

I guess you say, what can make me feel this way?

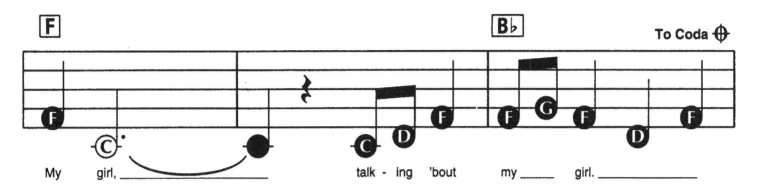

To Coda

My girl, _____ talk - ing 'bout my _____ girl. _____

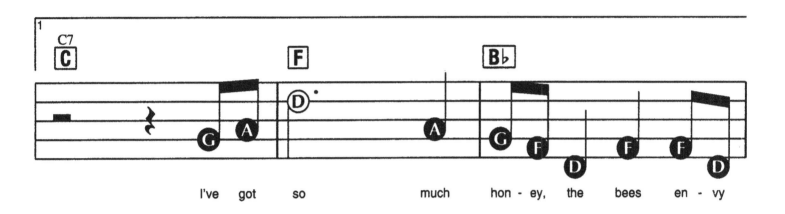

I've got so much hon - ey, the bees en - vy

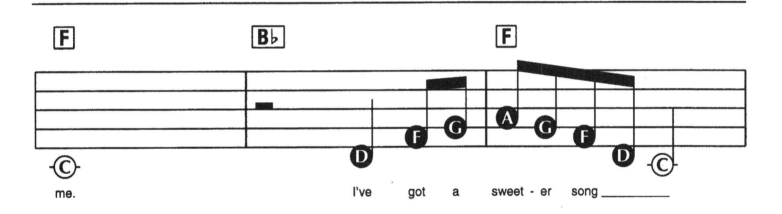

me. I've got a sweet - er song _____

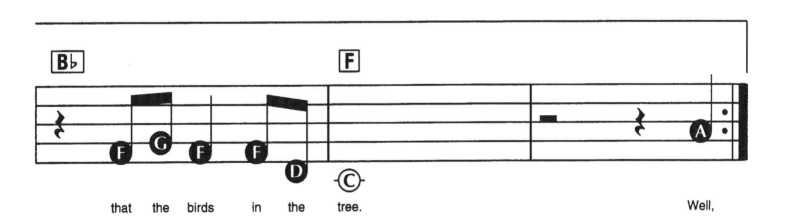

that the birds in the tree. Well,

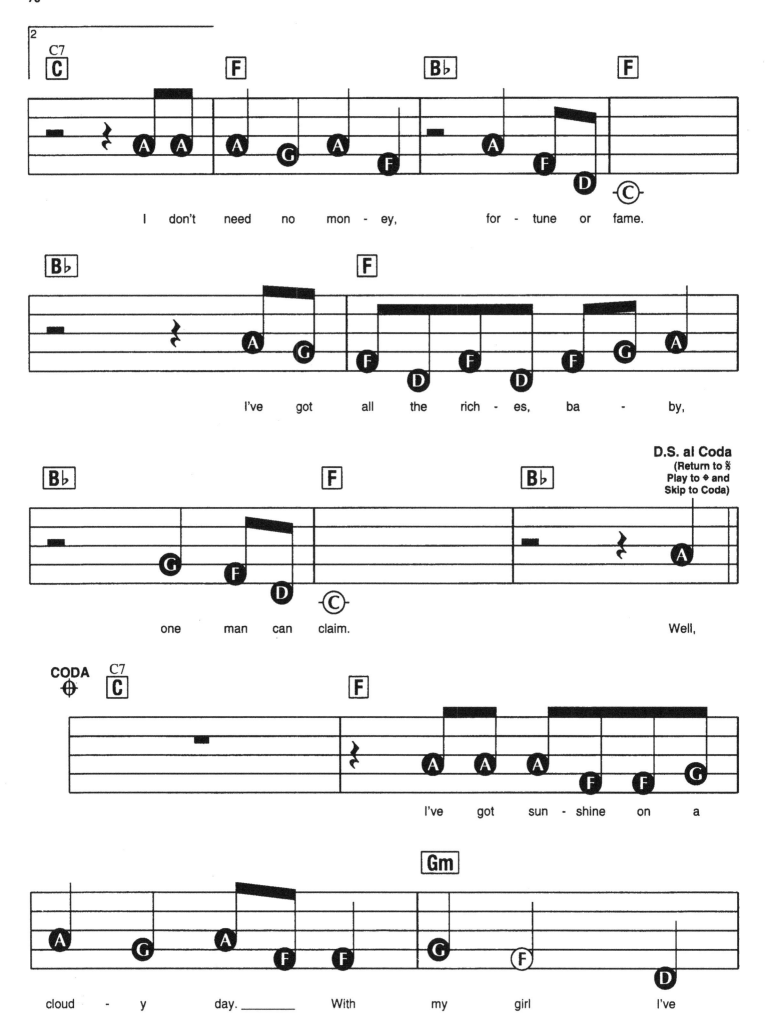

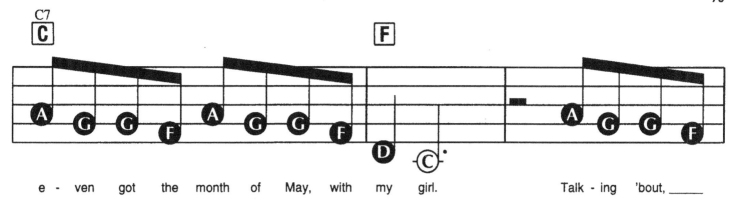

e - ven got the month of May, with my girl. Talk - ing 'bout, _____

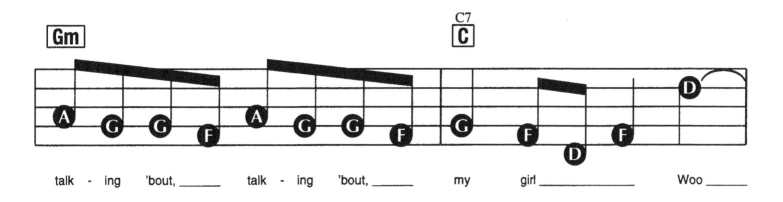

talk - ing 'bout, _____ talk - ing 'bout, _____ my girl _____ Woo _____

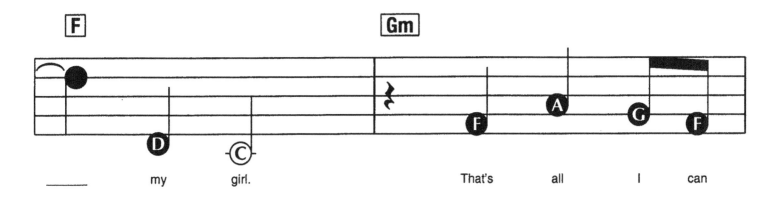

_____ my girl. That's all I can

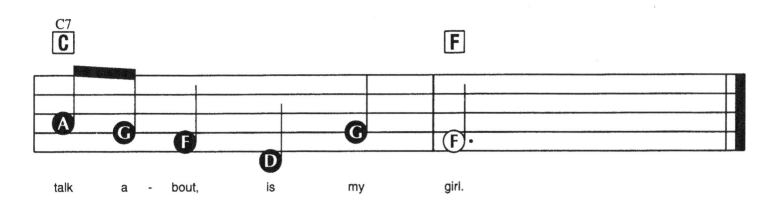

talk a - bout, is my girl.

(You've Got)
Personality

Registration 5
Rhythm: Shuffle or Swing

Words and Music by Lloyd Price
and Harold Logan

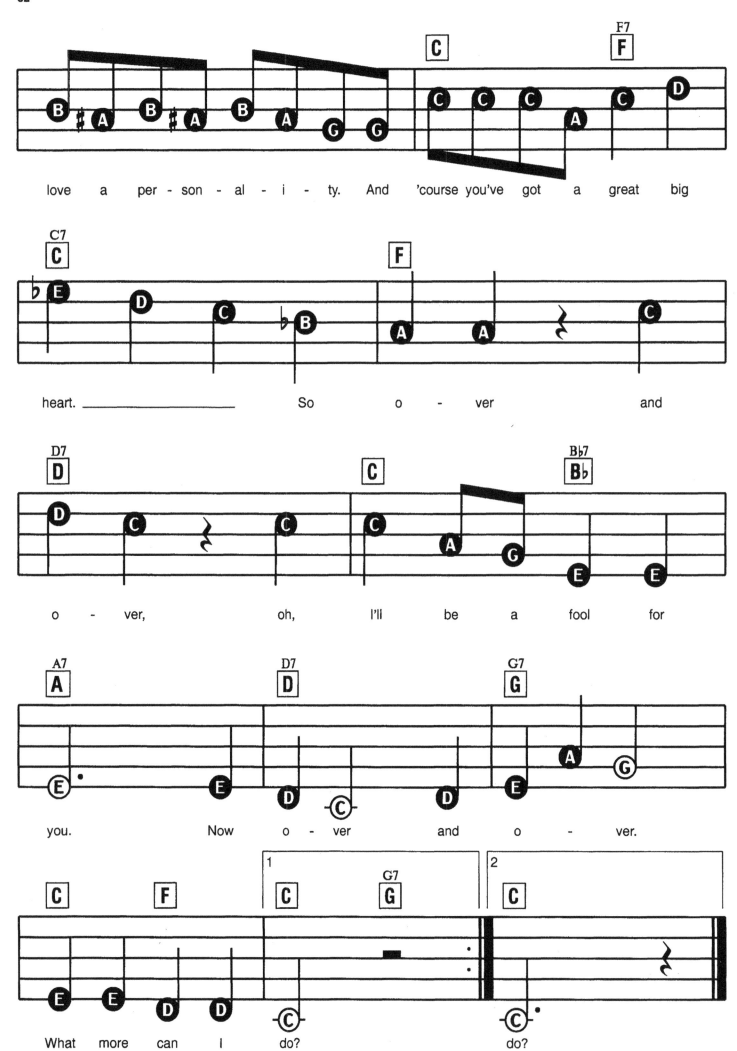

Respect

Registration 8
Rhythm: Rock

Words and Music by
Otis Redding

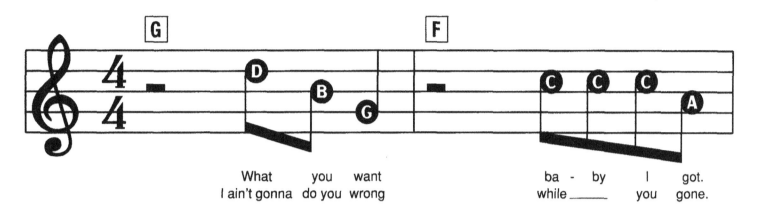

What   you   want   ba - by   I   got.
I ain't gonna do you wrong   while _____ you   gone.

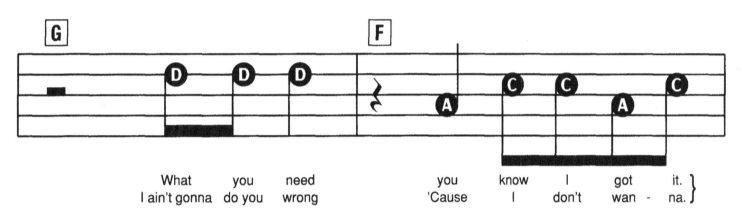

What   you   need   you   know   I   got   it.
I ain't gonna do you wrong   'Cause   I   don't   wan - na. }

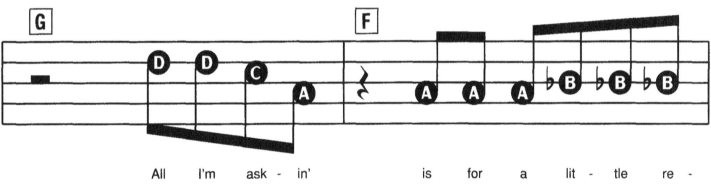

All   I'm   ask - in'   is   for   a   lit - tle   re -

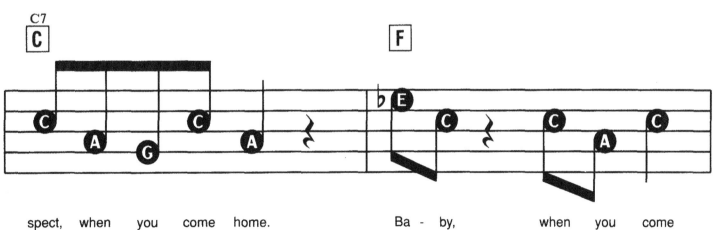

spect, when you come home.   Ba - by,   when you come

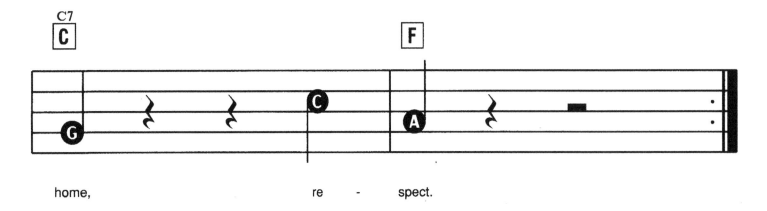

home,   re   -   spect.

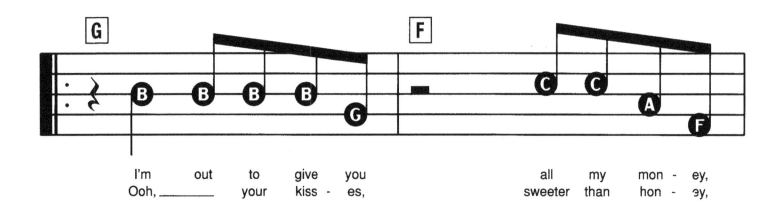

I'm   out   to   give   you   all   my   mon - ey,
Ooh, _____   your   kiss - es,   sweeter   than   hon - ey,

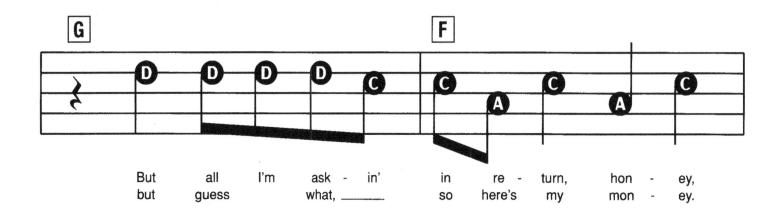

But   all   I'm   ask - in'   in   re - turn,   hon - ey,
but   guess   what, _____   so   here's   my   mon - ey.

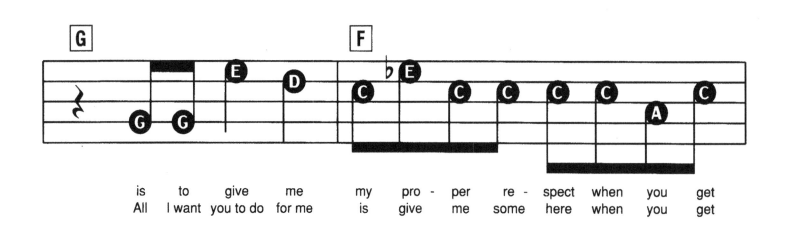

is   to   give   me   my   pro - per   re - spect   when   you   get
All   I want you to do for me   is   give   me   some   here   when   you   get

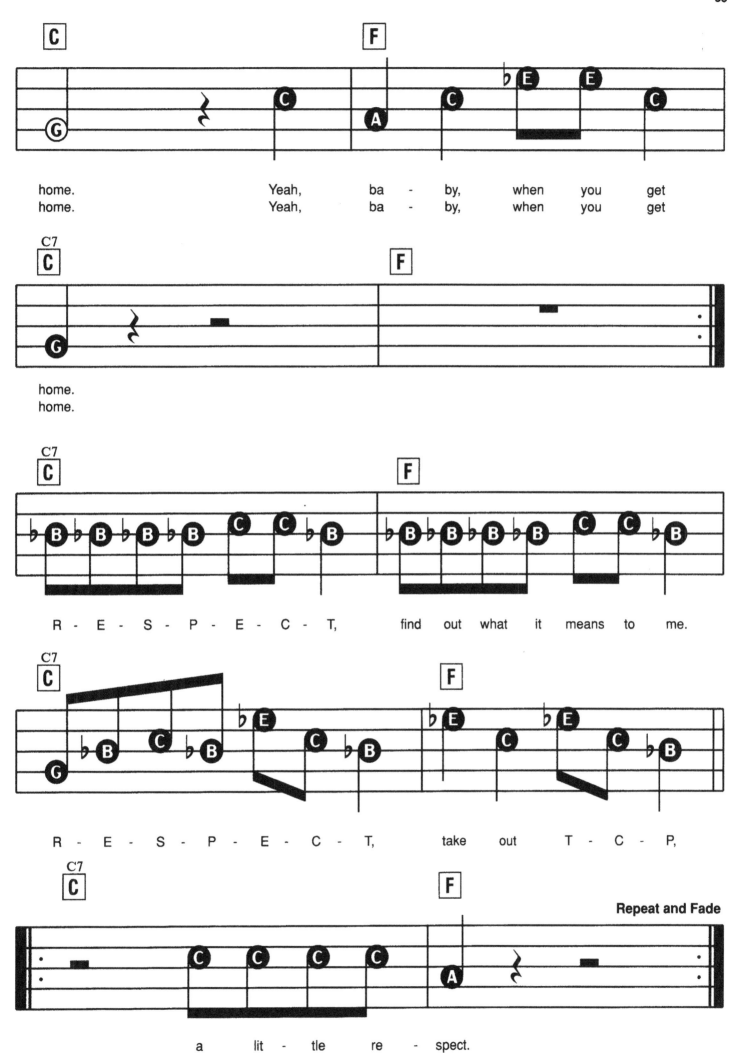

home.
home.

Yeah, ba - by, when you get
Yeah, ba - by, when you get

home.
home.

R - E - S - P - E - C - T, find out what it means to me.

R - E - S - P - E - C - T, take out T - C - P,

Repeat and Fade

a lit - tle re - spect.

Sheila

Registration 8
Rhythm: Rock 'n' Roll

Words and Music by
Tommy Roe

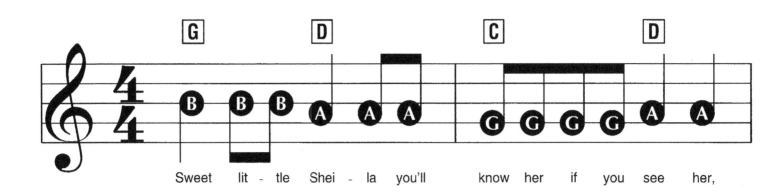

Sweet lit - tle Shei - la you'll know her if you see her,

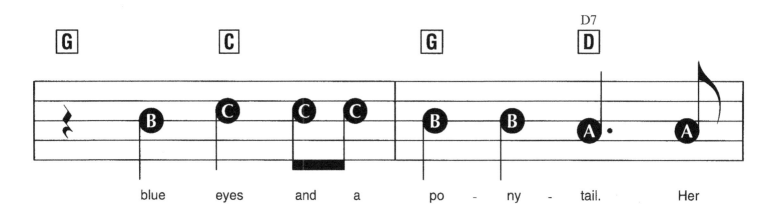

blue eyes and a po - ny - tail. Her

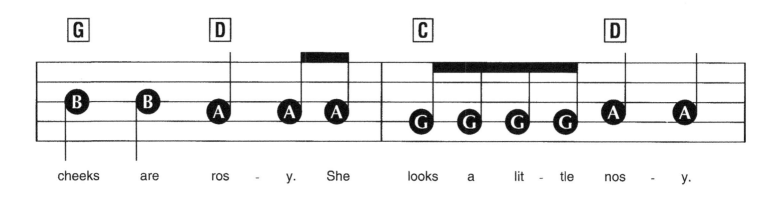

cheeks are ros - y. She looks a lit - tle nos - y.

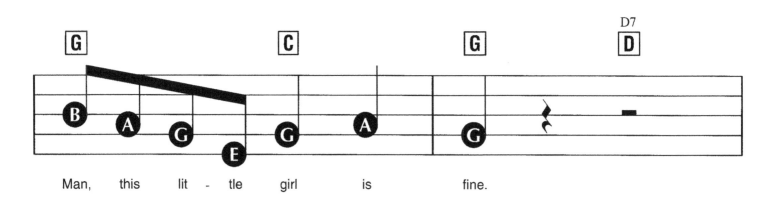

Man, this lit - tle girl is fine.

87

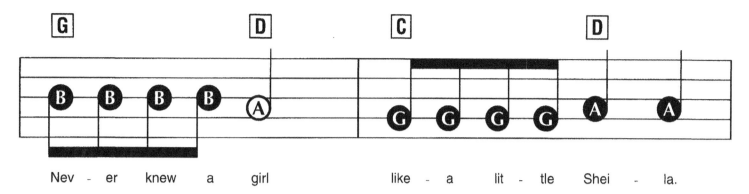

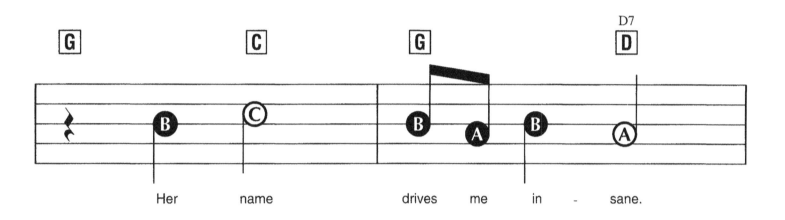

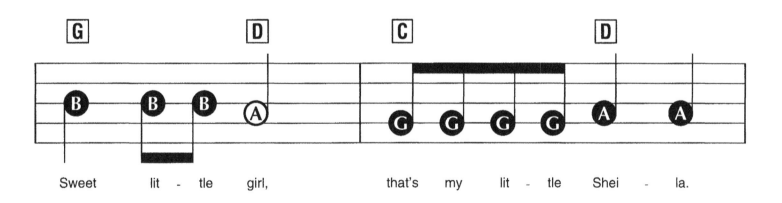

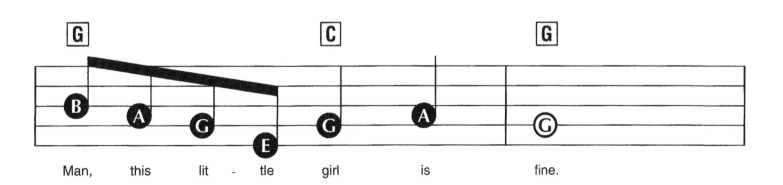

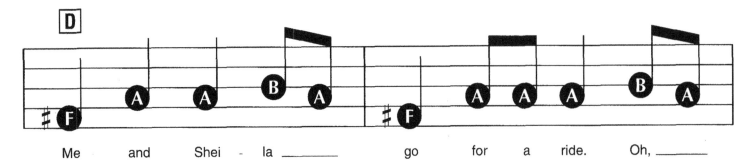

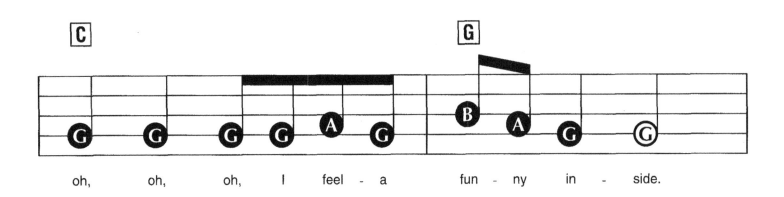

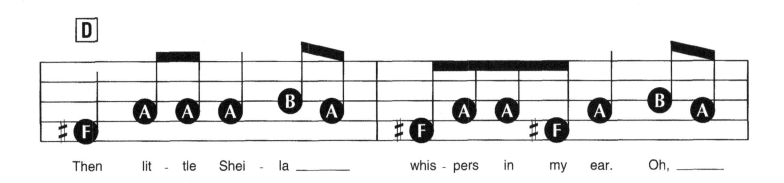

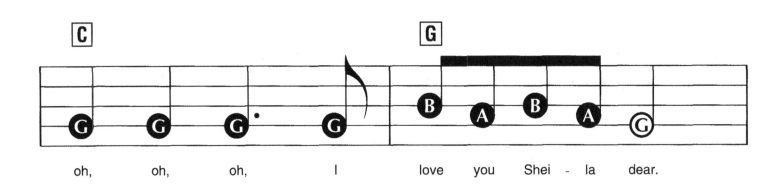

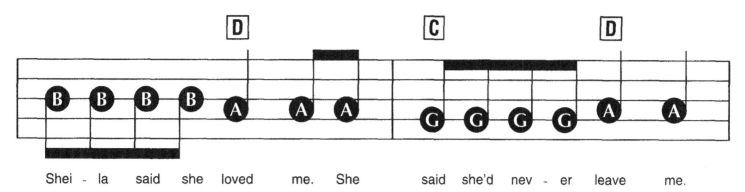

Shei - la said she loved me. She said she'd nev - er leave me.

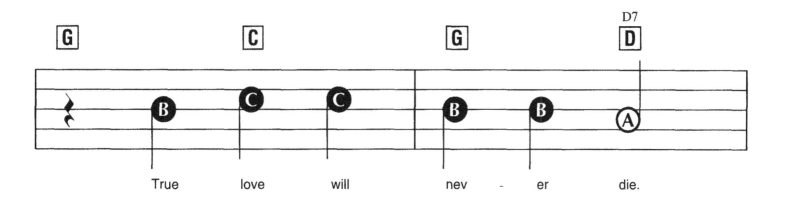

True love will nev - er die.

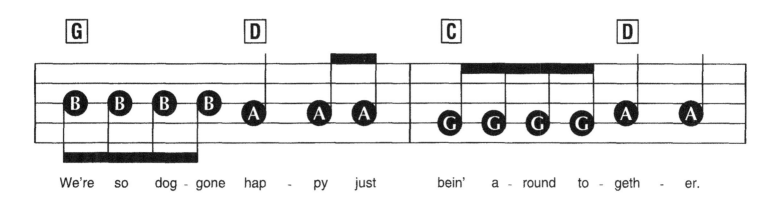

We're so dog - gone hap - py just bein' a - round to - geth - er.

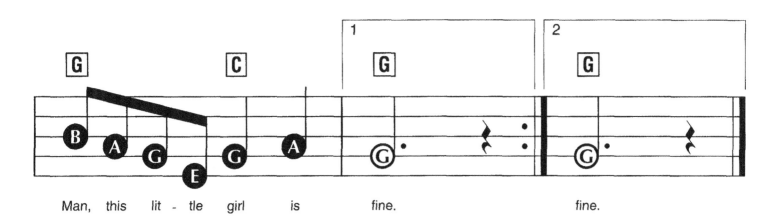

Man, this lit - tle girl is fine. fine.

Silence Is Golden

Registration 2
Rhythm: 8 Beat or Rock

Words and Music by Bob Crewe
and Bob Gaudio

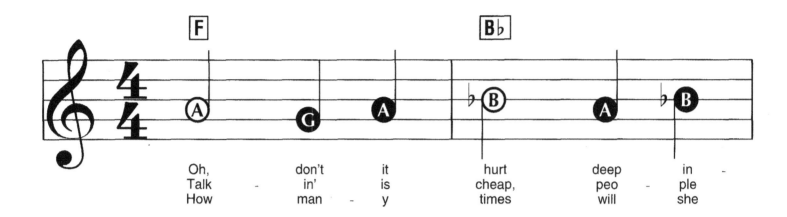

Oh,   don't   it   hurt   deep   in -
Talk - in'   is   cheap,   peo - ple
How   man - y   times   will   she

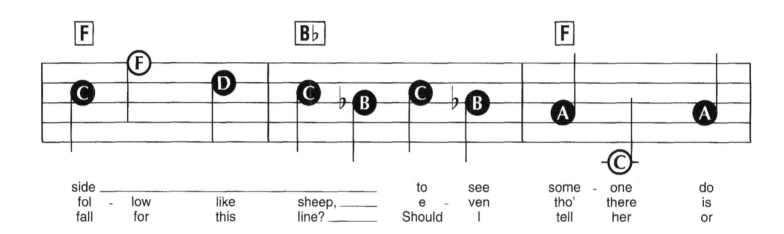

side _____ to   see   some - one   do
fol - low   like   sheep, ____ e - ven   tho'   there   is
fall   for   this   line? ____ Should   I   tell   her   or

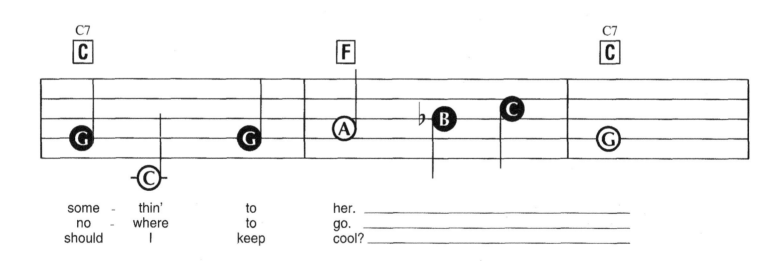

some - thin'   to   her. _____
no - where   to   go. _____
should   I   keep   cool? _____

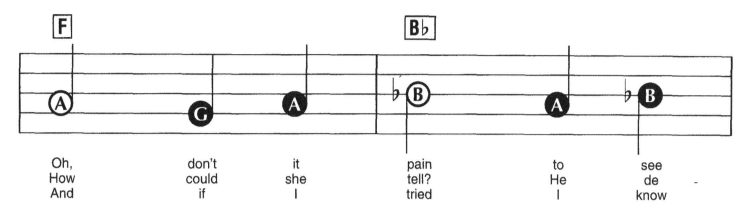

Oh,   don't   it   pain   to   see
How   could   she   tell?   He   de -
And   if   I   tried   I   know

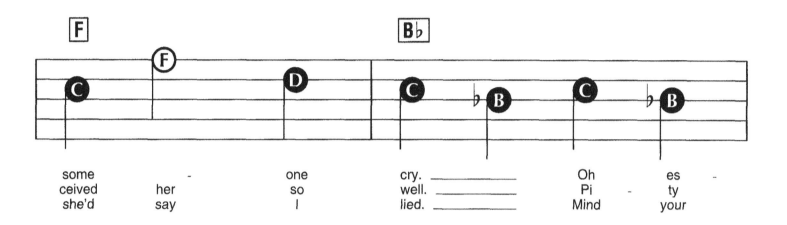

some -   one   cry. _____   Oh   es -
ceived her say so   well. _____   Pi -   ty
she'd   her say I   lied. _____   Mind   your

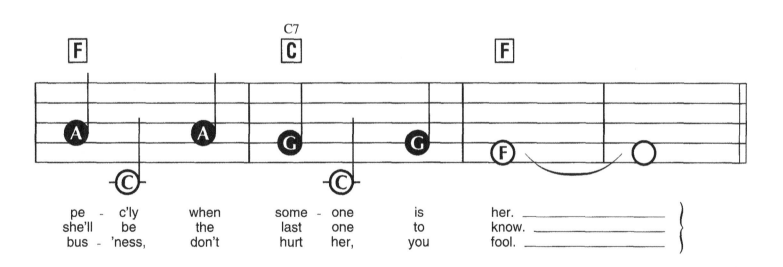

pe -   c'ly   when   some - one   is   her. _____
she'll be   the   last   one   to   know. _____
bus -   'ness,   don't   hurt   her,   you   fool. _____

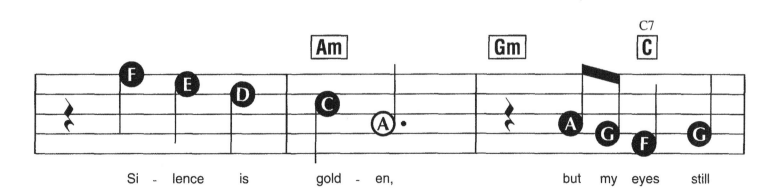

Si - lence is   gold - en,   but my eyes still

92

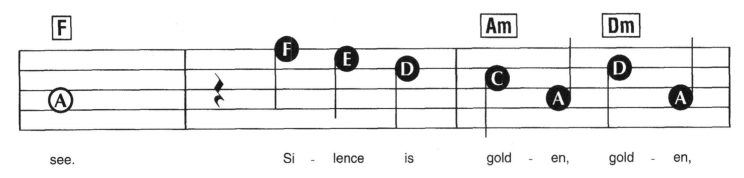

see. Si - lence is gold - en, gold - en,

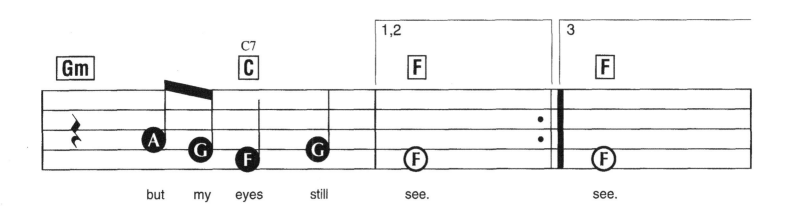

but my eyes still see. see.

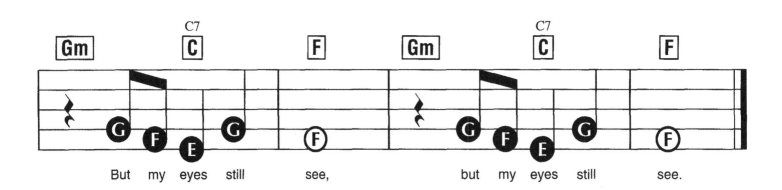

But my eyes still see, but my eyes still see.

Soldier Boy

Registration 8
Rhythm: 8 Beat or Rock

Words and Music by Luther Dixon
and Florence Green

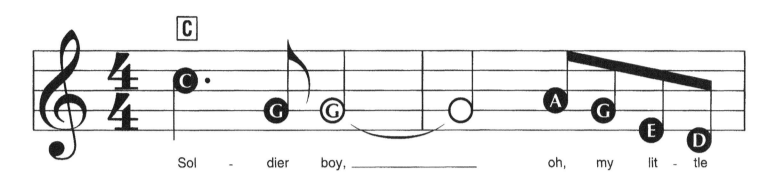

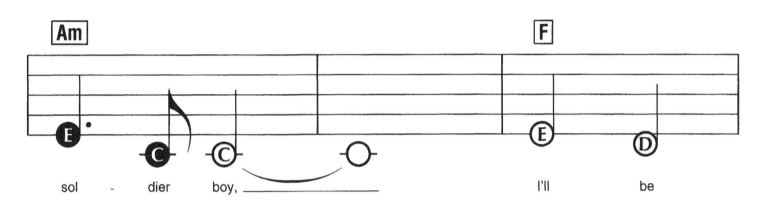

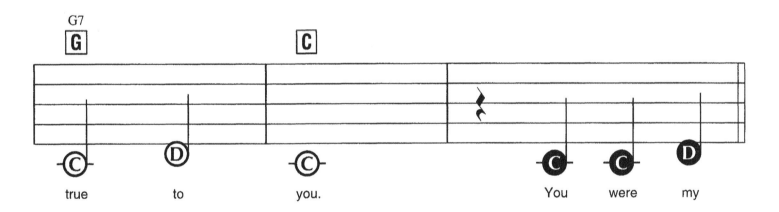

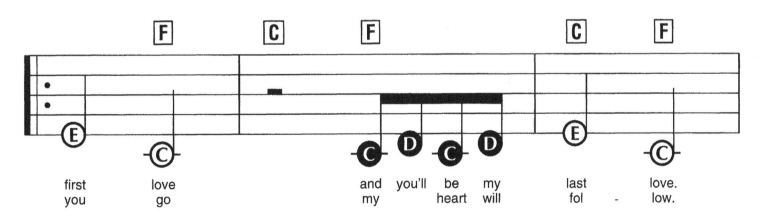

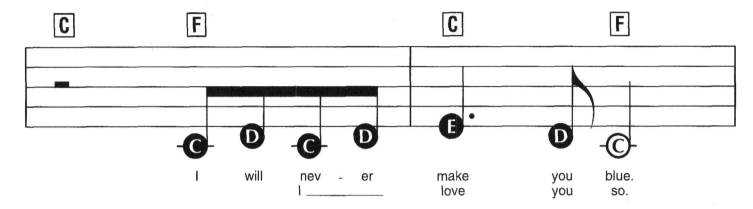

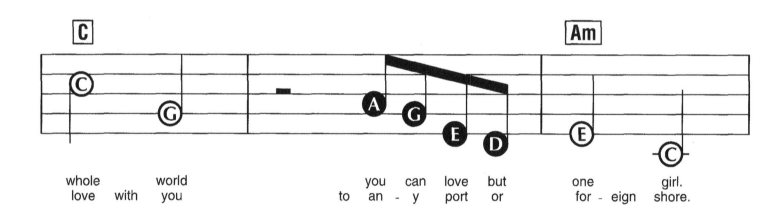

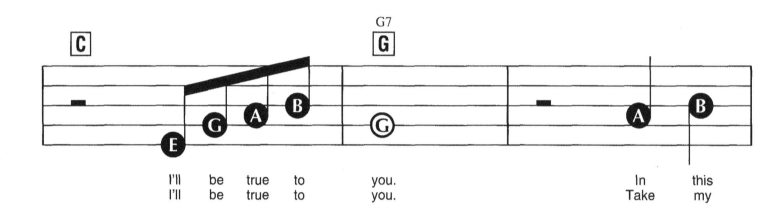

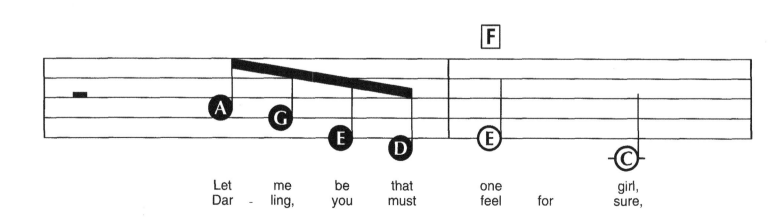

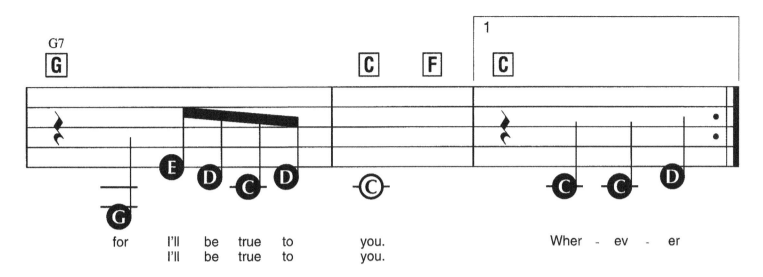

for I'll be true to you.
I'll be true to you.

Wher - ev - er

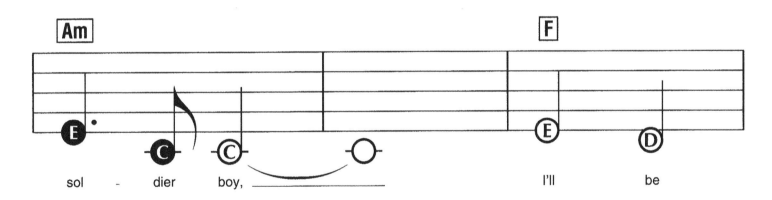

Sol - dier boy, oh, my lit - tle

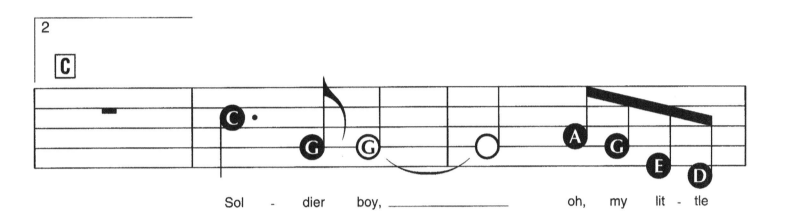

sol - dier boy, I'll be

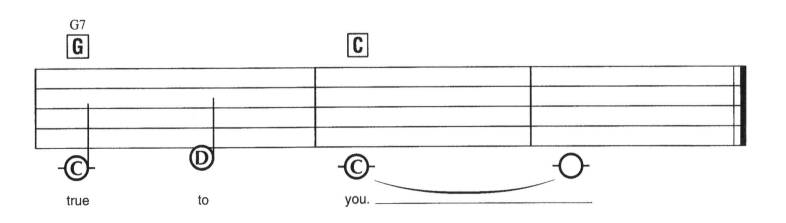

true to you.

Stagger Lee

Registration 5
Rhythm: Rock or Swing

Words and Music by Lloyd Price
and Harold Logan

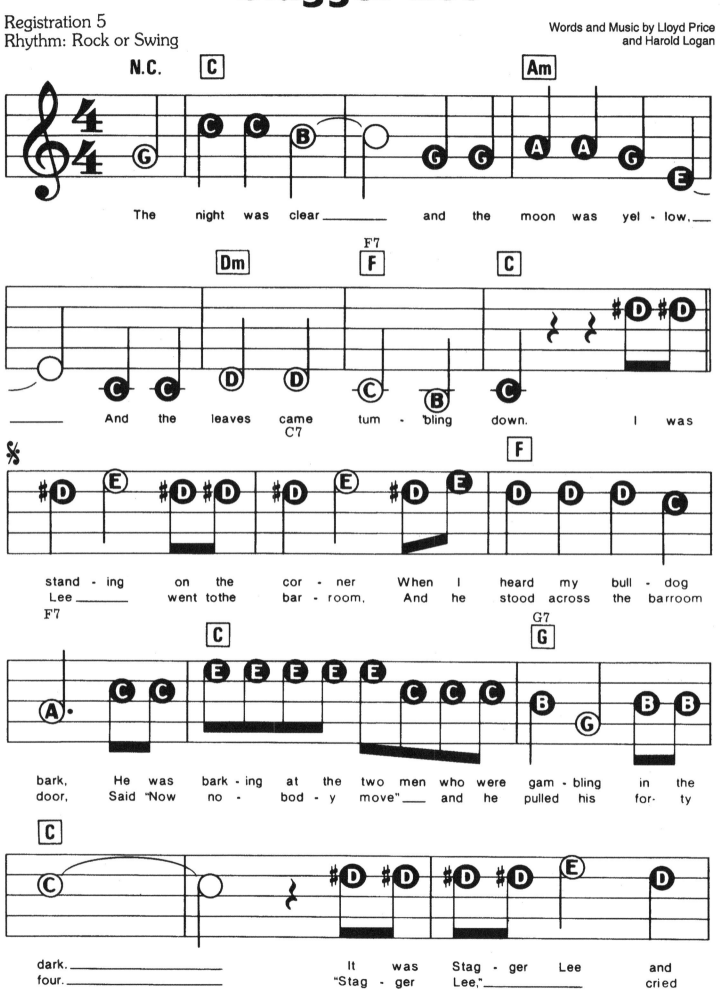

97

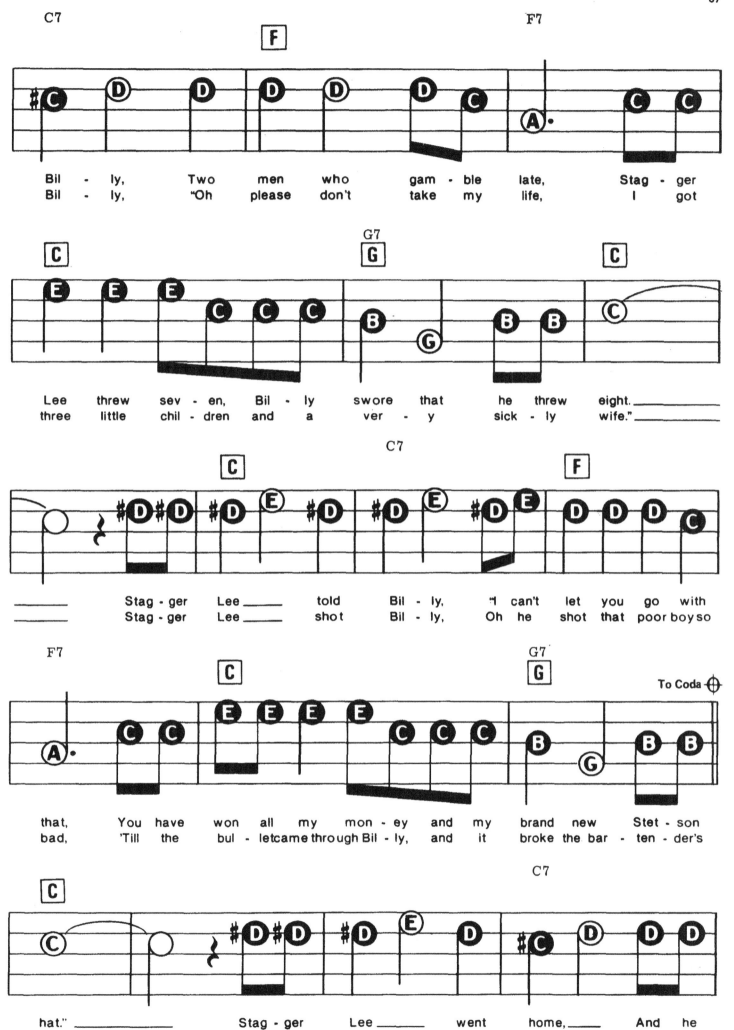

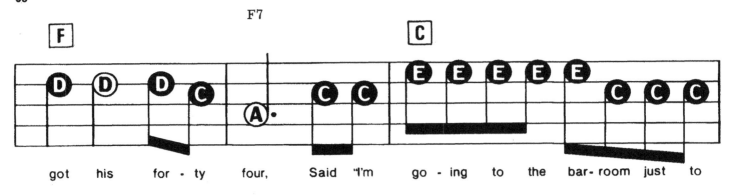

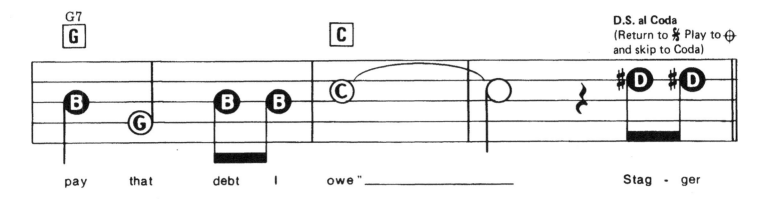

got his for - ty four, Said "I'm go - ing to the bar - room just to

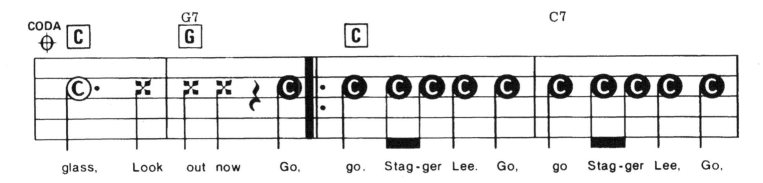

pay that debt I owe " _____ Stag - ger

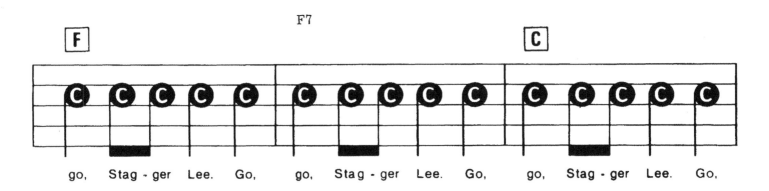

glass, Look out now Go, go. Stag -ger Lee. Go, go Stag -ger Lee, Go,

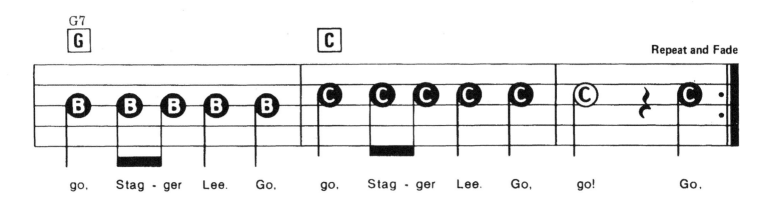

go, Stag - ger Lee. Go, go, Stag - ger Lee. Go, go, Stag - ger Lee. Go,

go, Stag - ger Lee. Go, go, Stag - ger Lee. Go, go! Go,

Stop! In the Name of Love

Registration 8
Rhythm: Rock or Pops

Words and Music by Lamont Dozier,
Brian Holland and Edward Holland

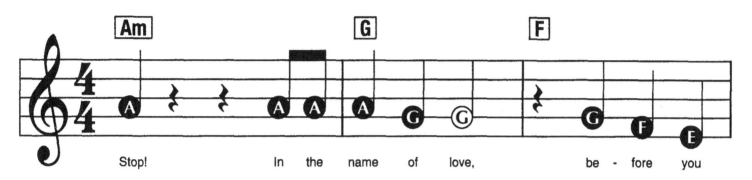

Stop! In the name of love, be - fore you

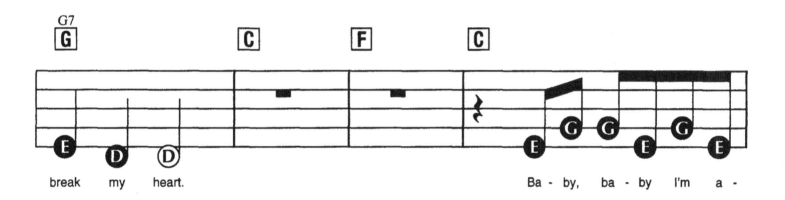

break my heart. Ba - by, ba - by I'm a -

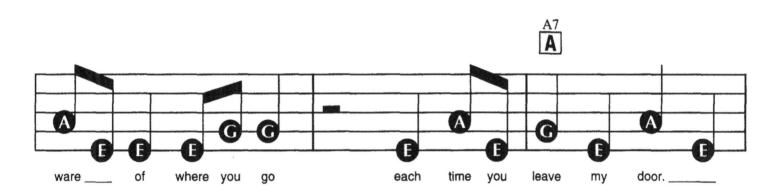

ware ___ of where you go each time you leave my door. _____

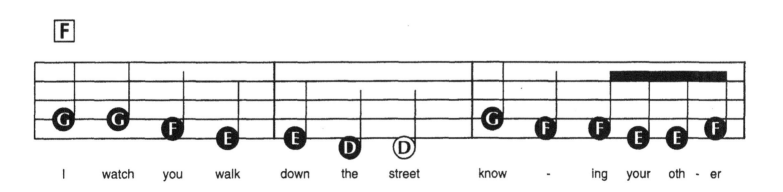

I watch you walk down the street know - ing your oth - er

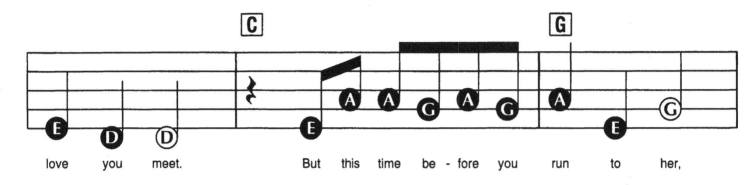

love   you   meet.   But   this   time   be - fore   you   run   to   her,

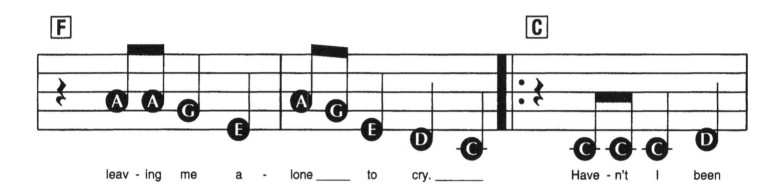

leav - ing   me   a - lone _____ to   cry. _____   Have - n't   I   been

good   to   you?   Have - n't   I   been   sweet _____ to   you? _____

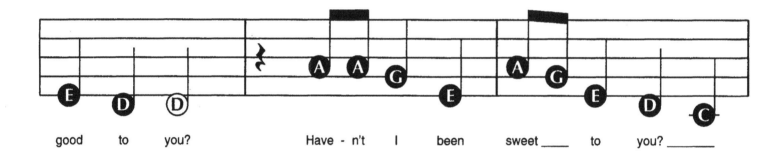

Stop!   In   the   name   of   love   be - fore   you

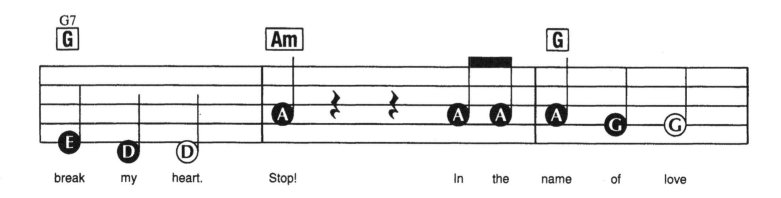

G7

break   my   heart.   Stop!   In   the   name   of   love

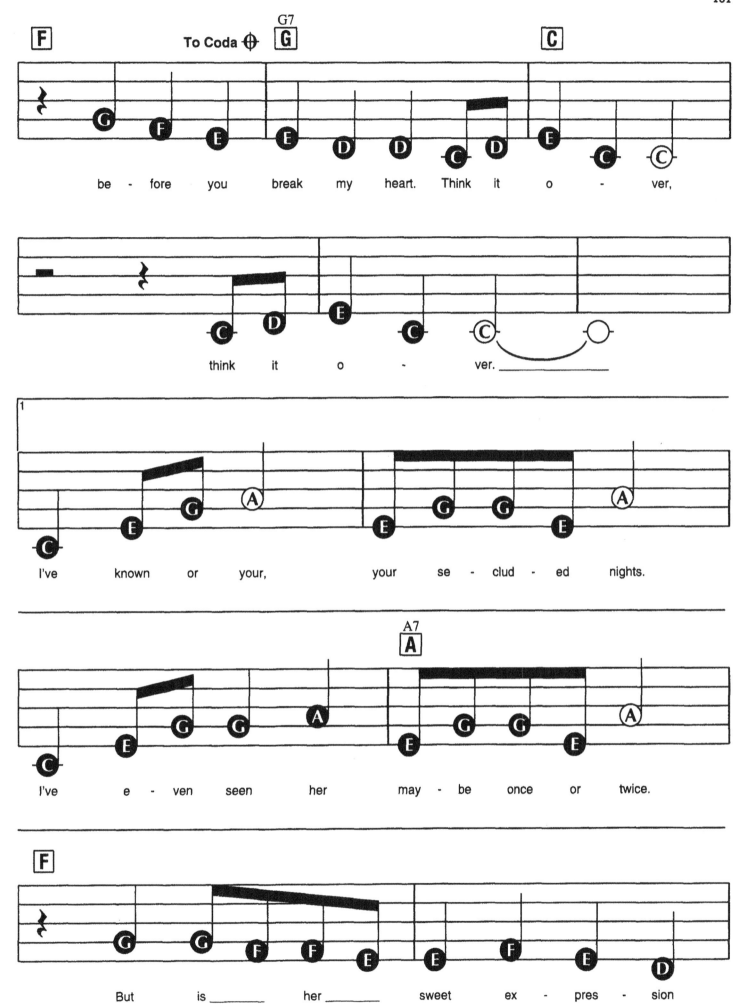

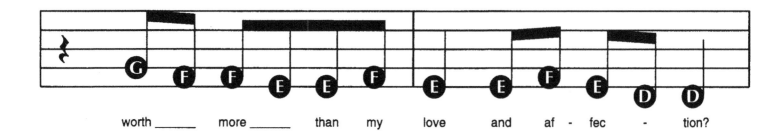

worth _____ more _____ than my love and af - fec - tion?

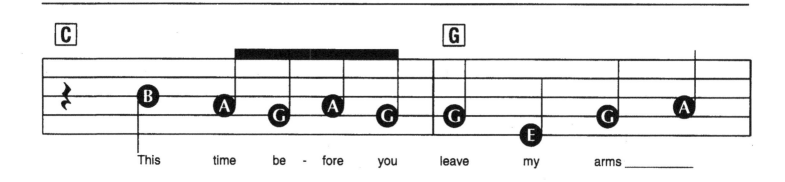

This time be - fore you leave my arms _____

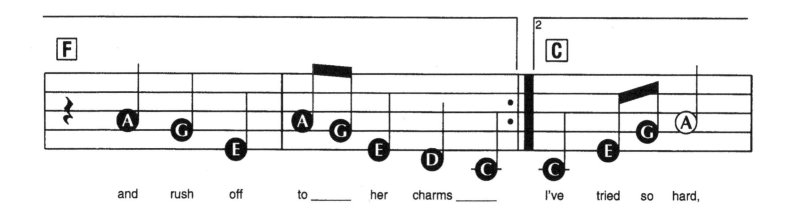

and rush off to _____ her charms _____ I've tried so hard,

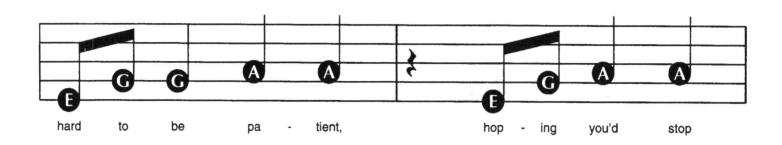

hard to be pa - tient, hop - ing you'd stop

103

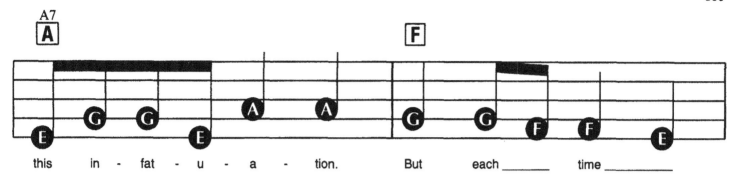

this in - fat - u - a - tion. But each _____ time _____

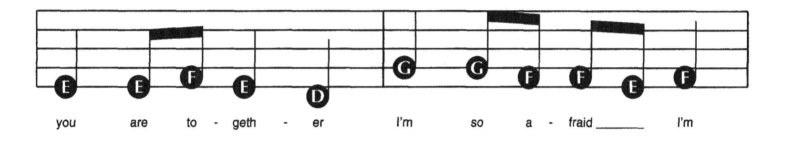

you are to - geth - er I'm so a - fraid _____ I'm

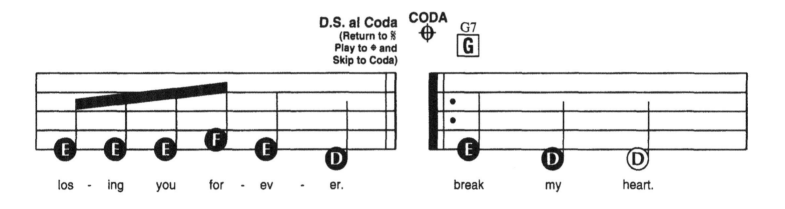

D.S. al Coda
(Return to %
Play to ⊕ and
Skip to Coda)

CODA ⊕

los - ing you for - ev - er. break my heart.

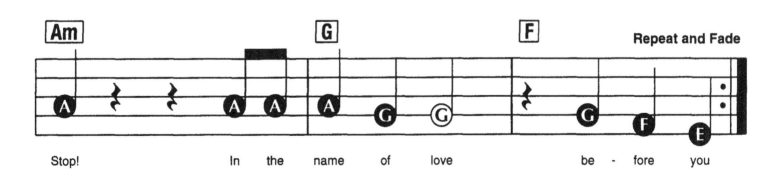

Repeat and Fade

Stop! In the name of love be - fore you

Stormy

Registration 8
Rhythm: 8 Beat or Rock

Words and Music by J.R. Cobb
and Buddy Buie

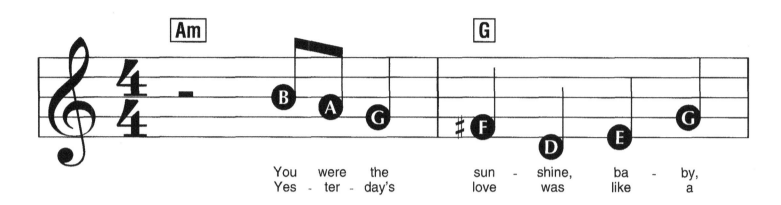

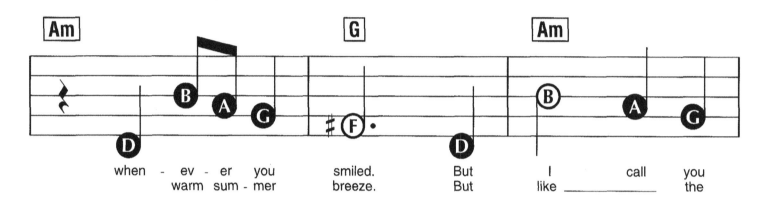

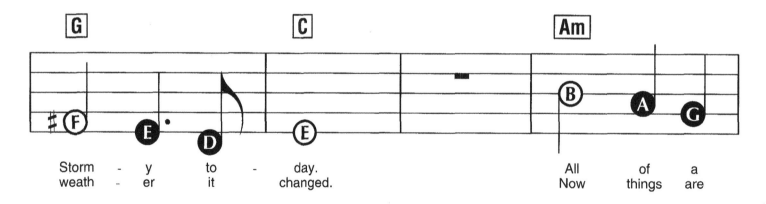

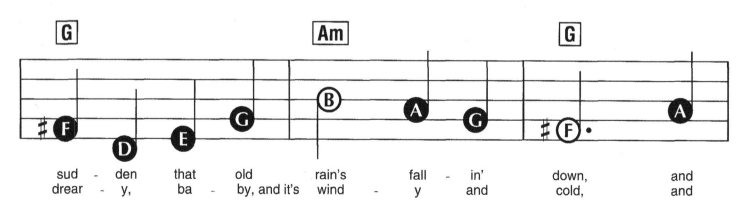

105

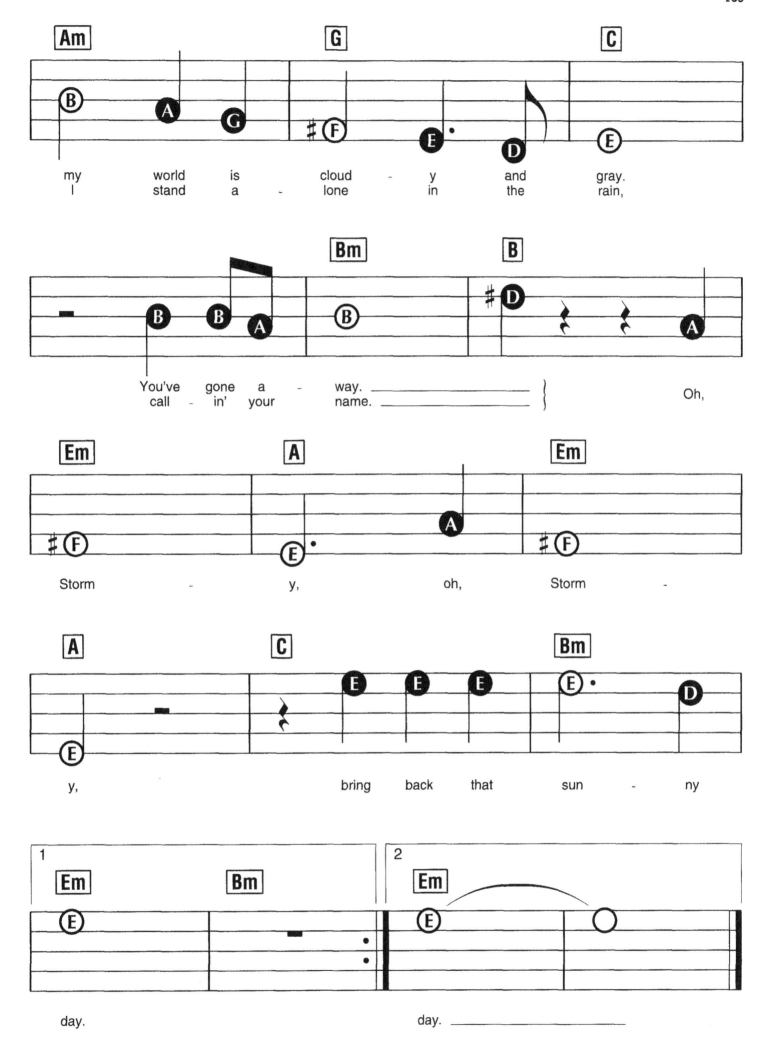

Tequila

Registration 8
Rhythm: Latin Rock or Rock

By Chuck Rio

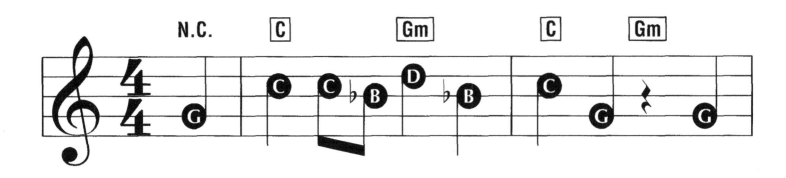

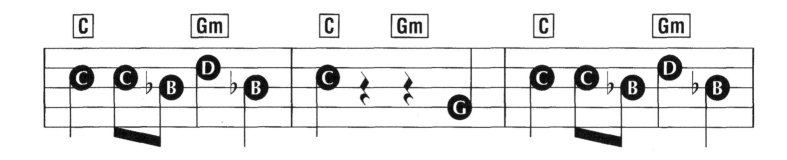

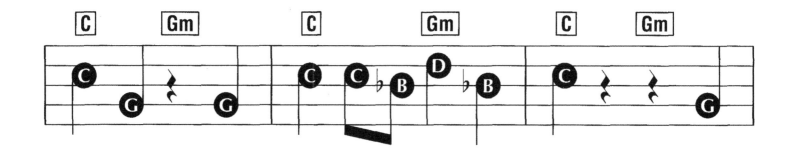

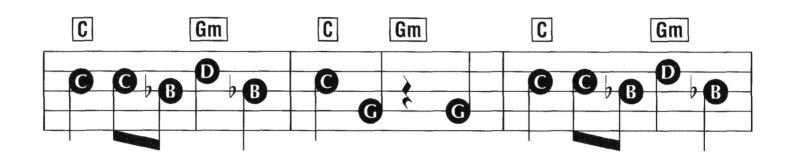

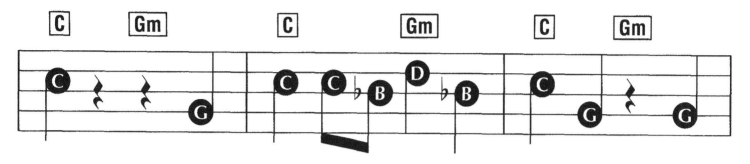

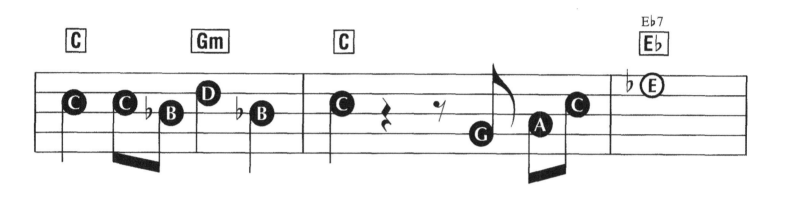

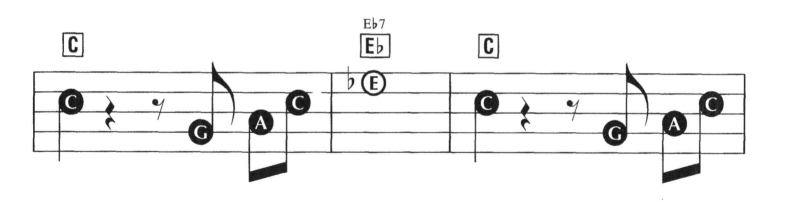

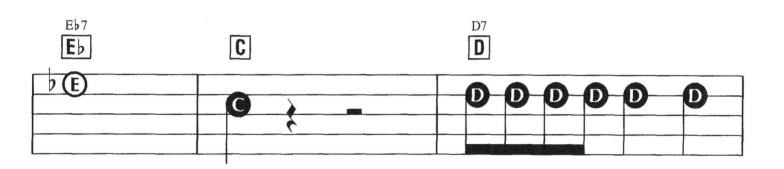

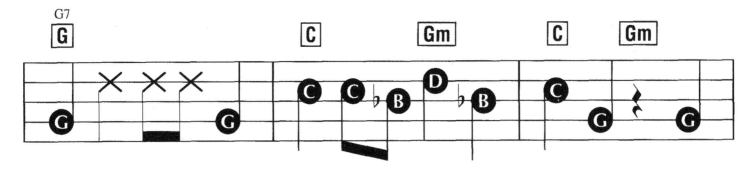

(Spoken:) Te - qui - la!

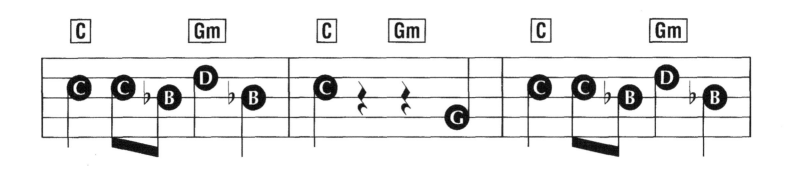

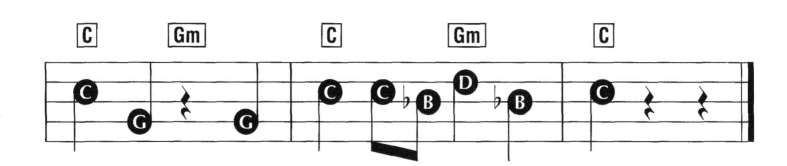

Travelin' Man

Registration 8
Rhythm: Country Rock or Rock

Words and Music by
Jerry Fuller

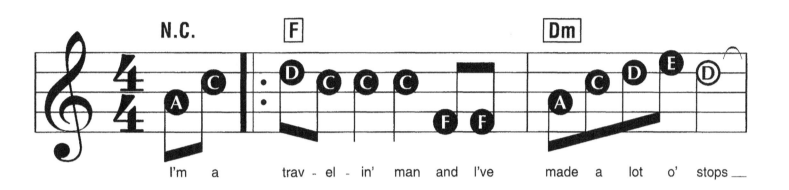

I'm a trav - el - in' man and I've made a lot o' stops ___

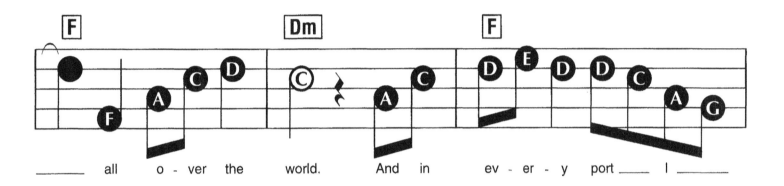

___ all o - ver the world. And in ev - er - y port ___ I ___

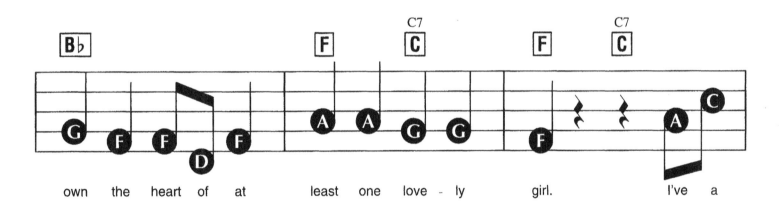

own the heart of at least one love - ly girl. I've a

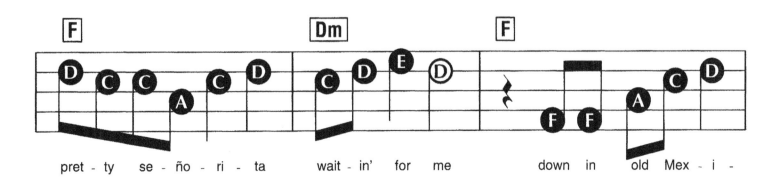

pret - ty se - ño - ri - ta wait - in' for me down in old Mex - i -

110

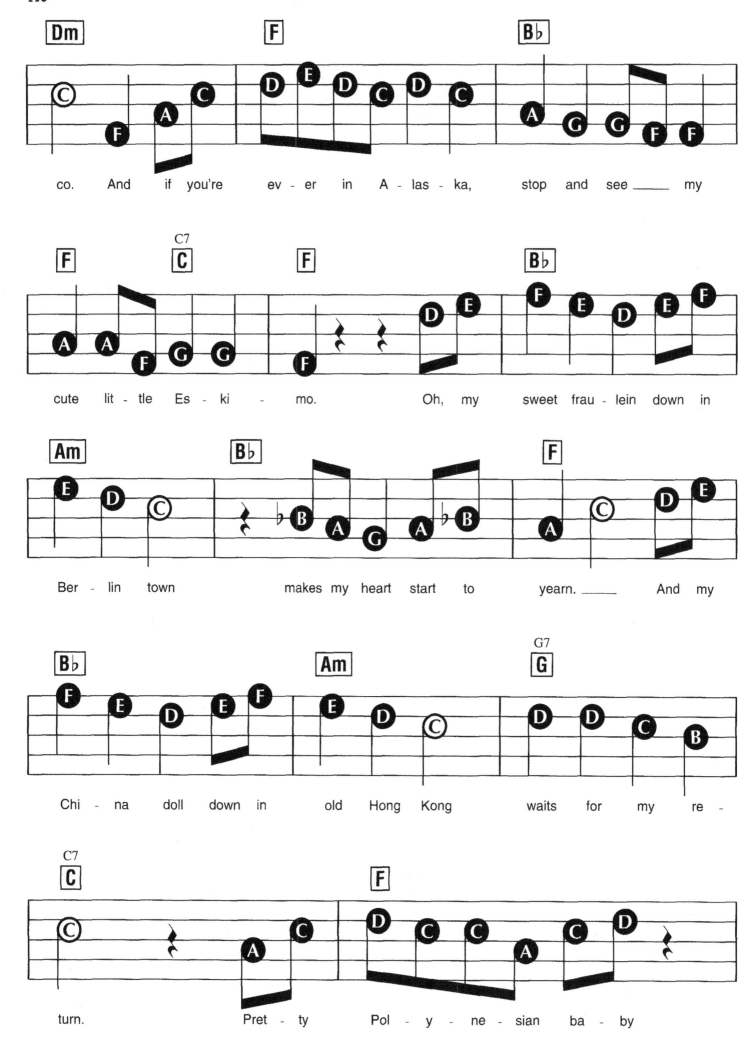

111

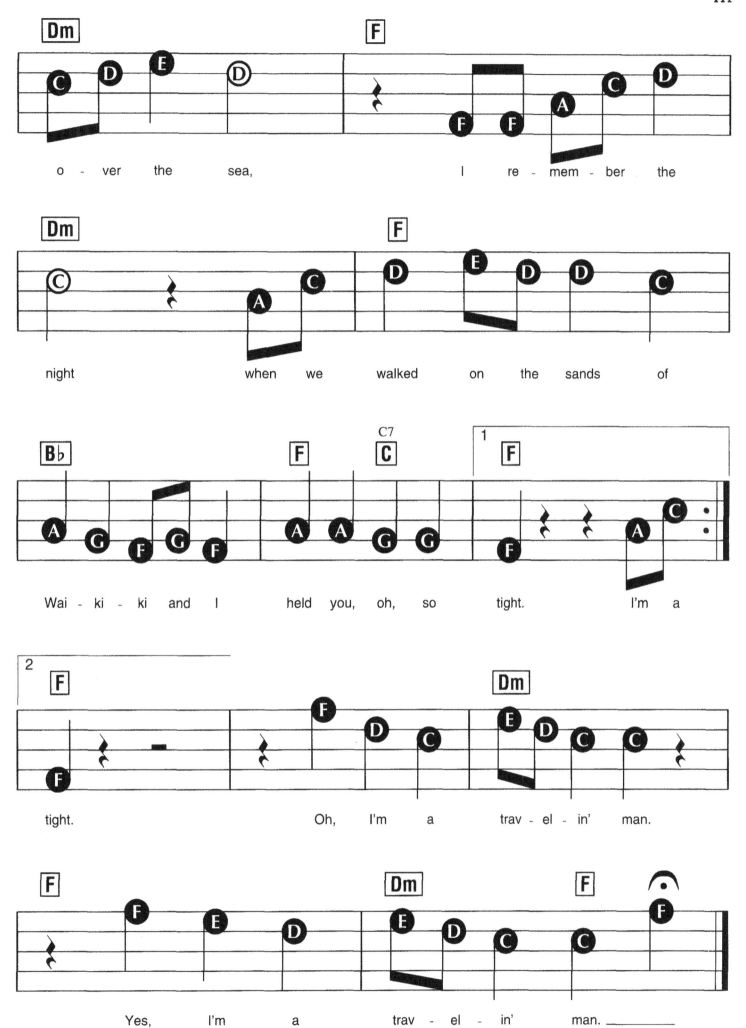

Walk Right In

Registration 7
Rhythm: 8 Beat or Rock

Words and Music by Gus Cannon
and H. Woods

Why Do Fools Fall in Love

Registration 8
Rhythm: Ballad

Words and Music by Morris Levy
and Frankie Lymon

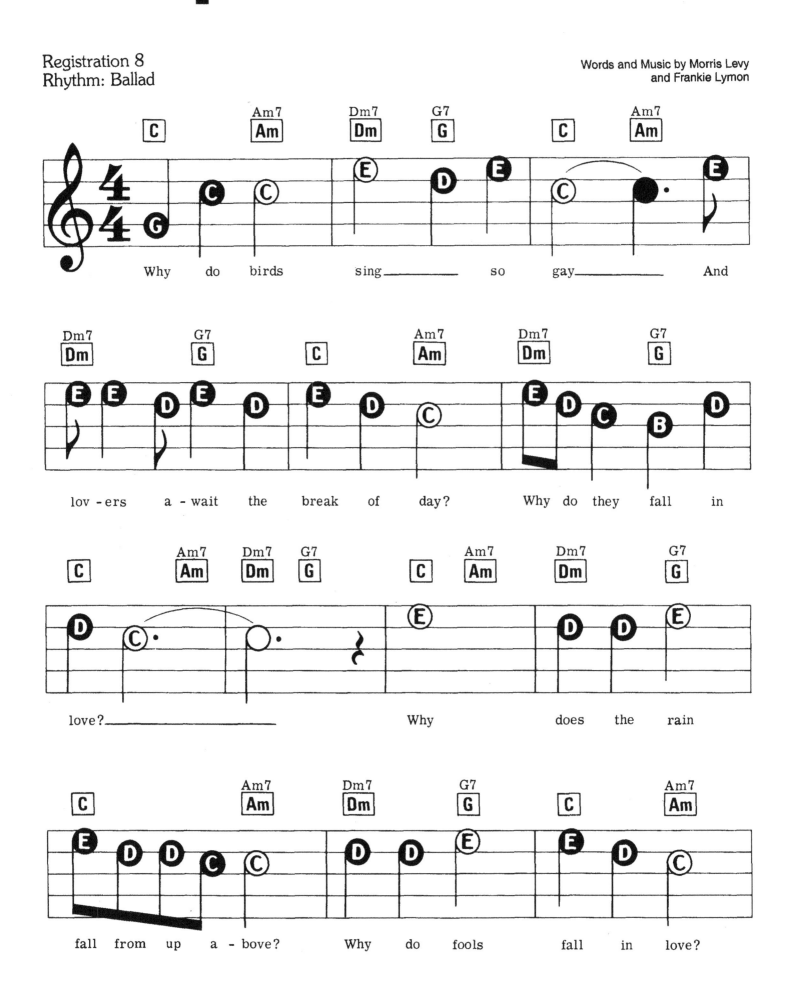

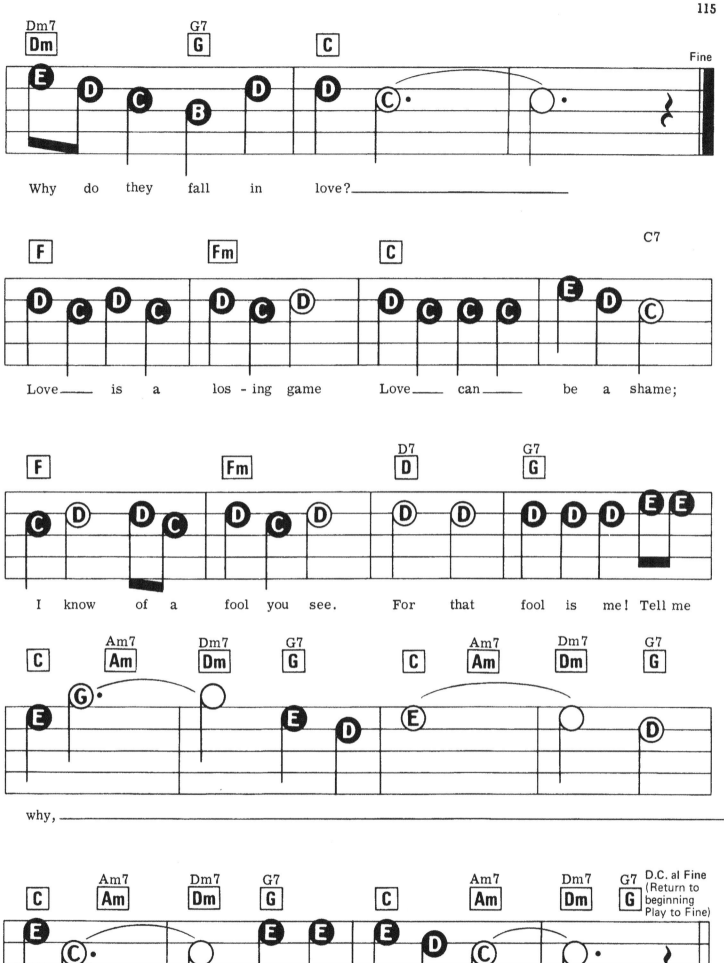

Winchester Cathedral

Registration 4
Rhythm: Fox Trot or Swing

Words and Music by
Geoff Stephens

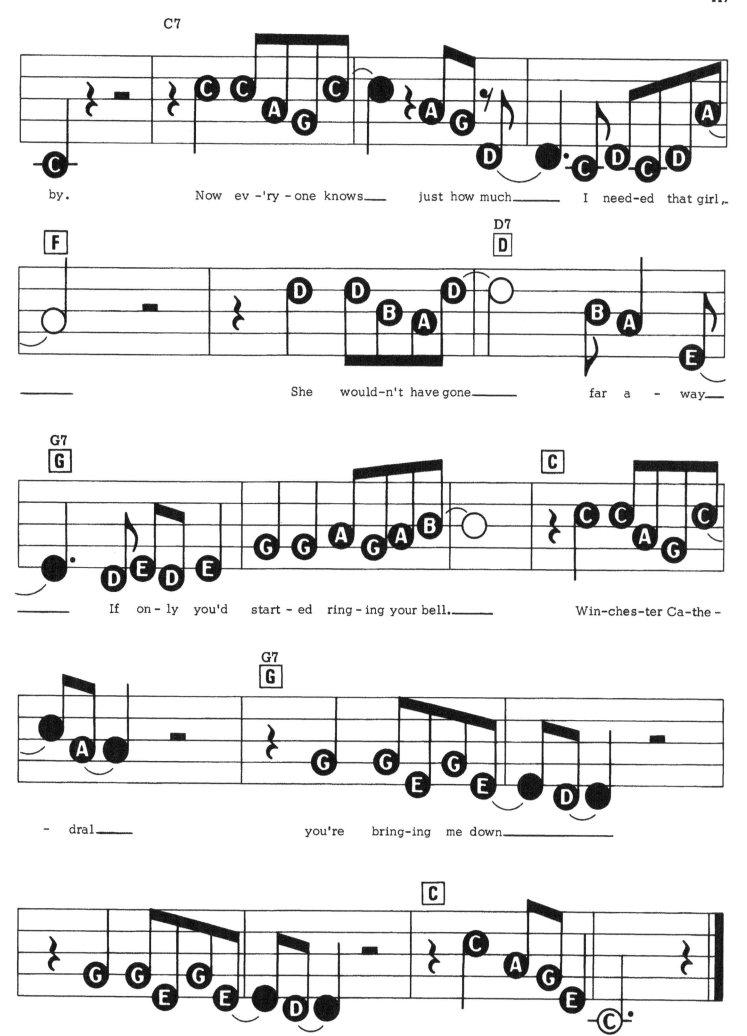

Windy

Registration 7
Rhythm: 8 Beat or Rock

Words and Music by
Ruthann Friedman

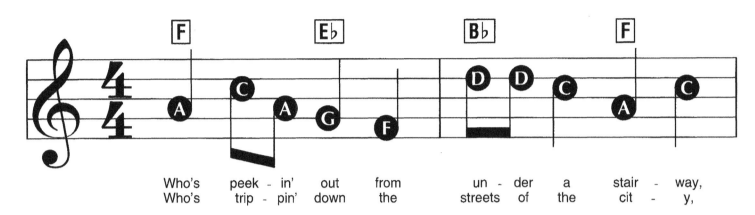

Who's peek - in' out from   un - der a stair - way,
Who's trip - pin' down from the   streets of the cit - y,

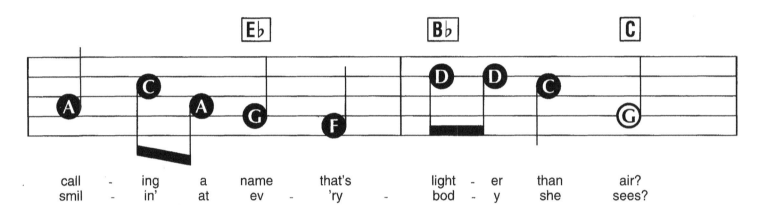

call - ing a name that's   light - er than air?
smil - in' at ev - 'ry - bod - y she sees?

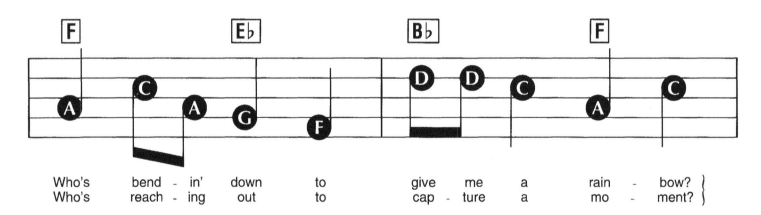

Who's bend - in' down to   give me a rain - bow?
Who's reach - ing out to   cap - ture a mo - ment?

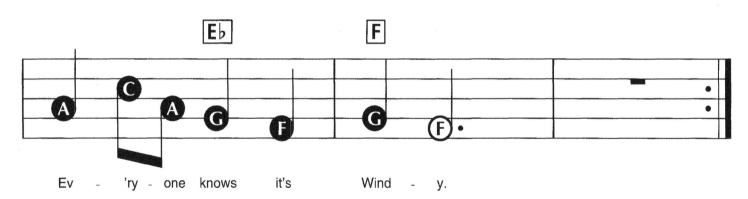

Ev - 'ry - one knows it's Wind - y.

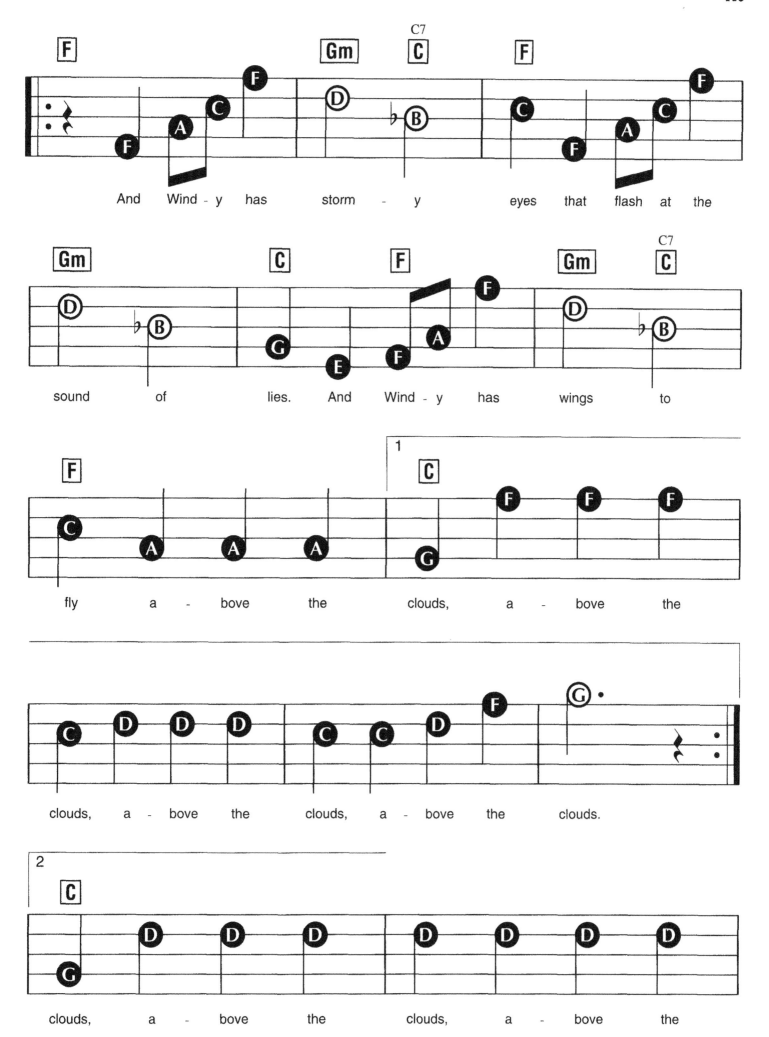

120

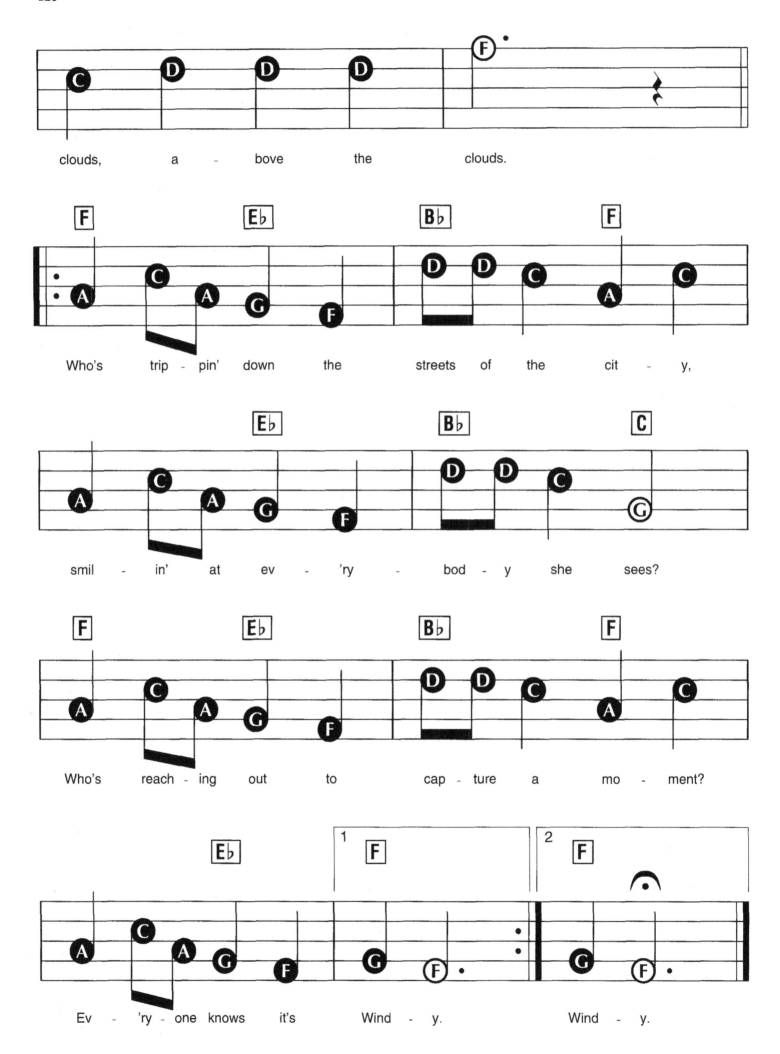

Wouldn't It Be Nice

Registration 8
Rhythm: Rock

Words and Music by Brian Wilson,
Tony Asher and Mike Love

122

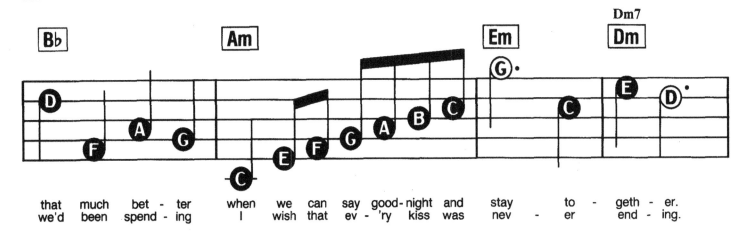

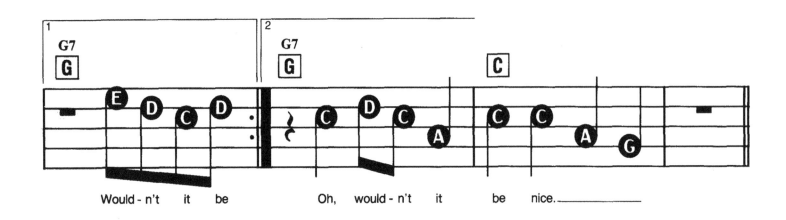

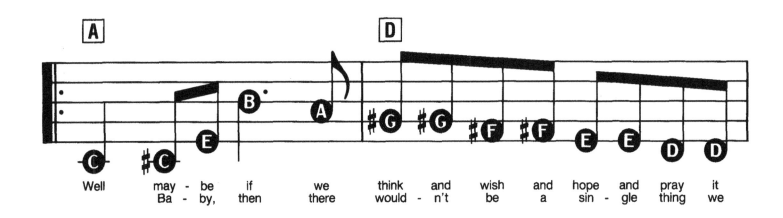

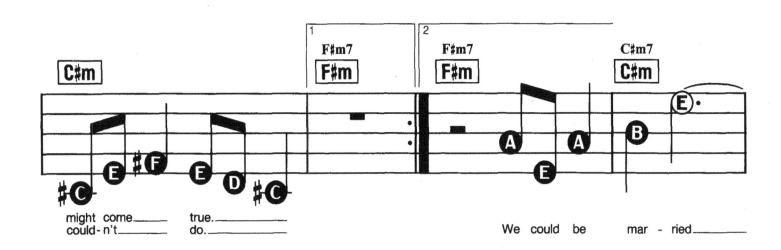

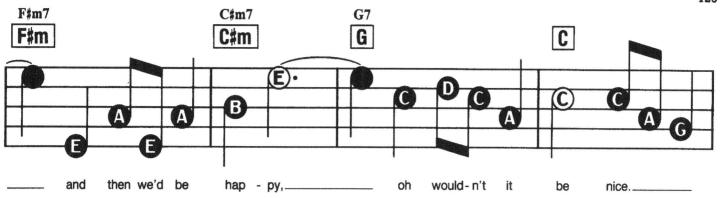

and then we'd be hap - py,_____ oh would-n't it be nice._____

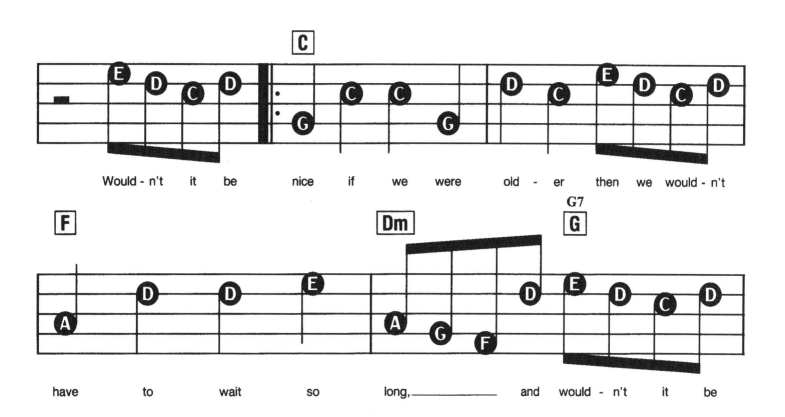

Would - n't it be nice if we were old - er then we would - n't

have to wait so long,_____ and would - n't it be

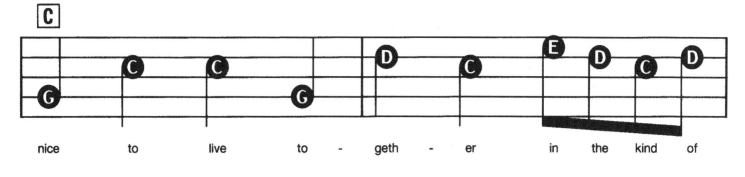

nice to live to - geth - er in the kind of

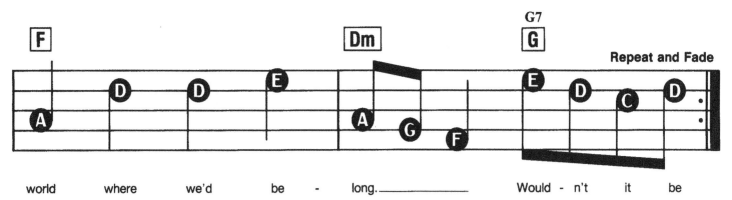

world where we'd be - long._____ Would - n't it be

You Keep Me Hangin' On

Registration 5
Rhythm: Rock or 8 Beat

Words and Music by Edward Holland,
Lamont Dozier and Brian Holland

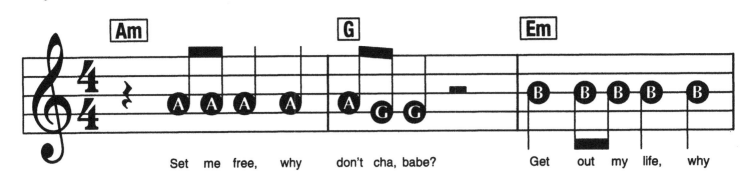

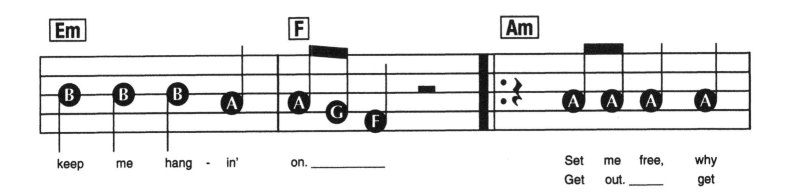

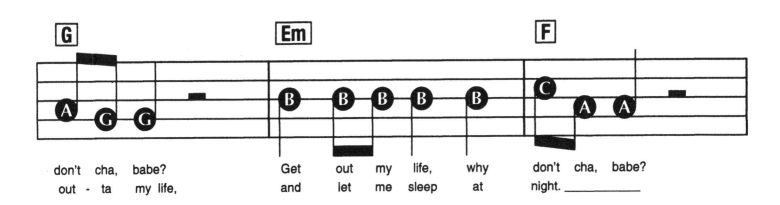

125

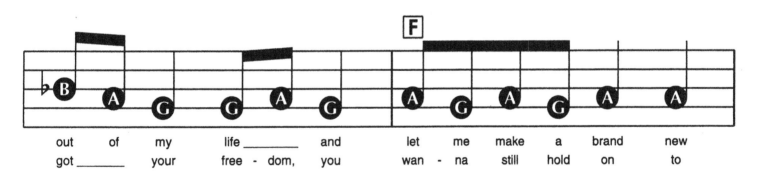

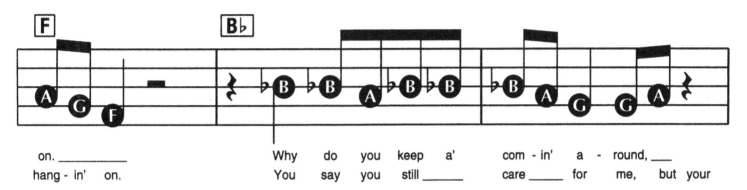

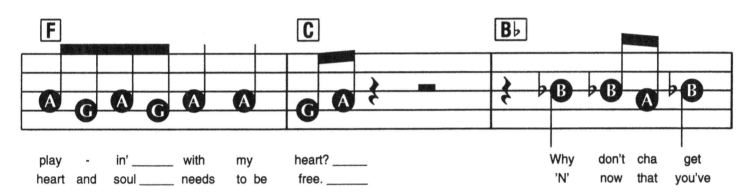

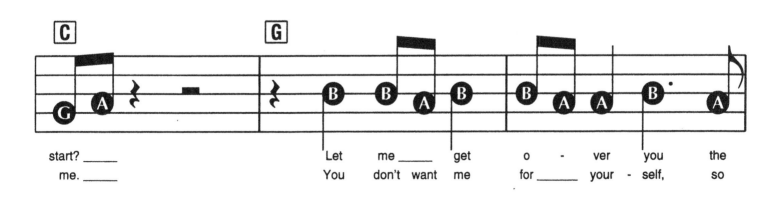

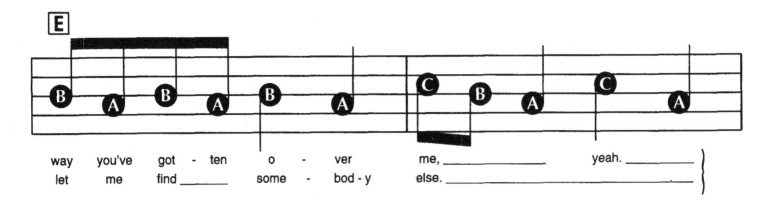

way you've got - ten o - ver me, _____ yeah. _____
let me find _____ some - bod - y else. _____

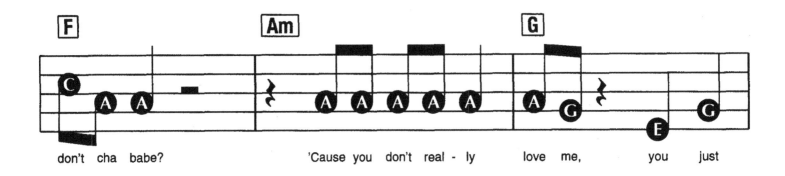

Set me free, why don't cha, babe? Get out my life, why

don't cha babe? 'Cause you don't real - ly love me, you just

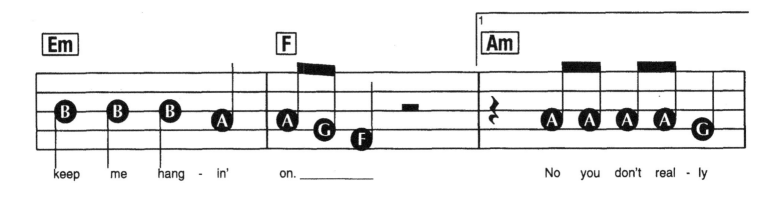

keep me hang - in' on. _____ No you don't real - ly

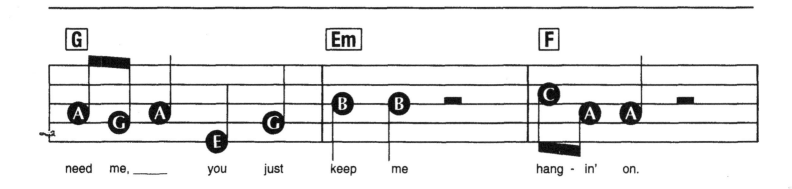

need me, _____ you just keep me hang - in' on.